Britain's Orchids

A guide to the identification
and ecology of the wild orchids
of Britain and Ireland

David Lang

ENGLISH
NATURE   **WILD**Guides

First published 2004 by **WILD**Guides Ltd.

WILDGuides Ltd.
Parr House
63 Hatch Lane
Old Basing
Hampshire
RG24 7EB
www.wildguides.co.uk

ISBN 1-903657-06-7

© 2004 David Lang
  Design, digital artwork and illustrations: Rob Still
  Maps: Rob Still, based on data collected by the BSBI Centre for Ecology and
  Hydrology and published in *The New Atlas of the British and Irish Flora* (OUP 2002)

  Edited by Andy Swash (**WILD**Guides) and Dr Jill Sutcliffe (English Nature)
  Project managed by Dylan Walker (**WILD**Guides)

The Wildlife Trusts partnership is the UK's leading conservation charity exclusively dedicated to wildlife. Our network of 47 local Wildlife Trusts and our junior branch, Wildlife Watch, work together to protect wildlife in towns, and the countryside, coastline and seas.

The Wildlife Trusts care for over 2,560 nature reserves from rugged coastline to urban wildlife havens. With more than 560,000 members, 26,000 volunteers, and unparalleled grass roots expertise, The Wildlife Trusts lobby for better protection of the UK's natural heritage and are dedicated to protecting wildlife for the future.

The vast array of nature reserves scattered throughout Britain include some of the very best places to see orchids growing in their natural habitats. The Wildlife Trusts is represented by a nationwide network of 47 local Wildlife Trusts caring for over 2,560 nature reserves. These reserves include some of the best orchid sites in the country, with management to ensure the protection of the orchids and the other wildlife special to each site. In addition, many reserves have excellent facilities, including visitor centres and nature trails, as well as events and guided walks, with local experts on hand to explain all about the orchids and other wildlife on show. The Wildlife Trusts can be contacted at:

The Wildlife Trusts, The Kiln, Waterside, Mather Road, Newark, Nottinghamshire NG24 1WT
Tel.: 0870 0367711; Fax: 0870 0360101 www.wildlifetrusts.org

The contact details for all local Wildlife Trusts can be found on pages 182–185 or on the following website: www.wildlifetrusts.org/index.php?section=localtrusts

Production and design by **WILD**Guides Ltd, Old Basing, Hampshire.
Printed in England by Apollo Print Management Ltd., Corby, Northamptonshire.

Contents

Species of uncertain or doubtful provenance

ENGLISH NATURE

Places where wildlife lives have been under great pressure in recent decades. Many species of plants and animals have been declining, and loss of habitat amounts to an area the size of the county of Shropshire every ten years. English Nature advises government on wildlife issues and is funded by the Department for Environment, Food and Rural Affairs. The organisation works to champion wildlife and to redress the balance by:

◆ overseeing a system of protected sites and wildlife legislation;
◆ introducing suitable management practices;
◆ devising and implementing wildlife-friendly policies;
◆ working in partnership with a range of people and organizations; and
◆ providing scientifically-based, sustainable solutions.

Some of the improvements being made can be seen in increases in populations and the range of both Red Kites and Otters, legal protection for species including the Water Vole and Great Crested Newt, the re-introduction of the Large Blue Butterfly, which was declared extinct in the UK in 1979, and an increased awareness of the importance of plants by safeguarding them and the sites where they grow. Orchids have played their part in this process. We want people to understand and appreciate the importance of England's natural heritage, and produce a range of information which is available from:

English Nature, Northminster House, Peterborough PE1 1UA;
Telephone: 01733 455000; Fax: 01733 568834.

There are also 22 Local Team offices, details of which can be obtained by telephoning Northminster House or by obtaining a copy of English Nature Facts and Figures information guide free from the Enquiry Service: Tel.: **01733 455100.**

You can also learn more about us via the internet: **www.english-nature.org.uk**

WILD*Guides*

WILD*Guides* is a publishing company committed to supporting wildlife conservation through financial donations and the provision of professional services. We produce definitive, yet simple-to-use wildlife identification guides aimed at encouraging a greater awareness of the plants and animals around us, highlighting the need for their conservation.

WILD*Guides* was formed in 2000, when we published our first book *Birds, Mammals and Reptiles of the Galápagos Islands*. In 2003, we teamed up with English Nature to produce a series of books on Britain's wildlife. This is the fifth book in the series, our other titles being *Arable Plants – a field guide*, *Britain's Dragonflies*, *Britain's Butterflies* and *Whales and Dolphins of the European Atlantic*.

To date, **WILD***Guides* has donated almost £10,000 to conservation charities in Britain and around the world. The sale of this book will benefit The Wildlife Trusts, who do so much to conserve wildlife, including wild orchids, on their reserves. To find out more about **WILD***Guides* visit our website: **www.wildguides.co.uk** or contact us at:

WILD*Guides***, Parr House, 63 Hatch Lane, Old Basing, Hampshire RG24 7EB;**
Telephone: 07818 403678; Fax: 01256 818039.

Foreword

Orchids are a fascinating and beautiful group of plants. When asked, many people might conjure up images of large shapely flowers, resplendent amongst the vegetation of a tropical island or in a glasshouse. However, it is quite possible to come across these plants much closer to home – visiting a meadow in the Midlands, out on some Scottish sand dunes, walking through a Welsh wood or investigating an Irish bog.

Some may feel that the 50 or so orchids that are native to Britain and Ireland are not quite as glamorous as their tropical counterparts, but as the photographs in this book demonstrate, they are just as varied, just as beautiful, and just as deserving of our concern for their future.

A quick dip into the definitive text and you will also discover that many of our orchids have a fascinating past. Their history is all the more compelling because the current health of our orchid populations is a reflection of our centuries-old relationship with them. This relationship has often been to the detriment of the plants, but may yet prove to be to their benefit. It is no coincidence that our most magnificent orchid is also our rarest.

At the beginning of the 19th Century, the Lady's-slipper occurred widely in Yorkshire, Lancashire and County Durham. But these were the days of the great Victorian collectors, and the Lady's-slipper frequently fell foul of a trowel. Today, the last specimen occurring in the wild is the subject of an intense recovery programme, designed, not only to protect that single plant, but also to improve its chances of being seen by us and by our descendants.

Thankfully, our influence on Britain's orchids has not been entirely detrimental. We have established a network of protected sites and brought in laws designed to protect our plants. We also owe an enormous debt to that tremendous army of amateur botanists past and present. Not only have they spent countless hours studying and watching over these fabulous plants, but some 1,600 people contributed the data on which the maps included in this guide are based. These individuals, working closely with conservation staff, have contributed much to our understanding, thereby supporting our current conservation efforts.

This excellent field guide is a testament to the work of amateur orchid enthusiasts everywhere. It is also a symbol of the importance of encouraging peoples' interest in wildlife. The result is a fitting tribute to the efforts of the author, an amateur naturalist with a lifelong passion for these delightful plants, a passion which this book can only encourage in others.

Dr. Andy Brown
Chief Executive
English Nature

Introduction

Orchids have an enormous appeal to many people, whether they have a great interest in botany or not, their beauty and brilliant colours creating an instant impression. However, there is much more to orchids than sheer good looks: some have bizarre life-cycles and others are valuable indicators of the health of our environment.

Orchids form one of the largest families of flowering plants on our planet, with thousands of species distributed world-wide. Although the fifty or so species which grow in Britain may form but a tiny part of the picture, our orchids are every bit as fascinating as their more flamboyant tropical cousins. They have inspired the passionate enthusiasm of botanists and writers alike for at least the last three hundred years. Shakespeare, for example, mentioned the Early-purple Orchid in 'Hamlet', where the Queen, speaking of the mad Ophelia, says:

Early-purple Orchids.

> *There with fantastic garlands did she come*
> *Of crowflowers, nettles, daisies and long purples:*
> *That liberal shepherds give a grosser name;*
> *But our cold maids do dead men's fingers call them.*

'Long purples' describes the flowering spike, while the shepherds were rudely referring to the two round tubers! Orchid flowers vary in shape from the beautiful to the bizarre. Close inspection of a flower spike may reveal florets resembling monkeys, lizards, bees, spiders or even human figures! However, evolution did not mould these weird and wonderful shapes by chance. Some of these masterpieces of mimicry attract insect pollinators by their shape, while others work by chemical deceit, secreting pheromones similar to those produced by the female insect.

Monkey Orchid flower-head.

The great Charles Darwin was particularly intrigued by this, and studied orchid pollination near his home at Downe in Kent. This led, in 1877, to the publication of his famous treatise *The Various Contrivances by which Orchids are Fertilised by Insects*. The flowers of some orchids exaggerate the most appealing features of the insect that they are trying to attract, effectively creating irresistible 'super-models' in petal form! The object of the deceit is achieved when the insect, sexually aroused, goes on to visit other flowers, thereby transferring pollen and ensuring cross-fertilisation. (See the section on *Reproduction and pollination* on *pages 14–15*, and the photograph of a Digger Wasp 'mating' with a Fly Orchid flower on *page 14*.)

Rare orchids have always been avidly sought after by collectors in the past. During the 18th and 19th Centuries this uncontrolled practice led to the decline of many species, and in some cases contributed to their extinction. Sadly, these thoughtless acts continue even today, their effects compounded by the large-scale intensification of agriculture and by the loss of habitat which has taken place throughout Britain since the Second World War.

I have been fortunate indeed to have been able to pursue an interest in orchids for most of my life. It all started at school, where I discovered an old book in the biology laboratory library which contained beautiful watercolour illustrations of British orchids. I found them fascinating for their colours and bizarre shapes, and secretly vowed that one day I would find all the British and Irish species, a vow which took me more than thirty years to fulfil and involved travelling to every corner of these islands.

My first 'find' was common enough – Early-purple Orchid in a damp wood just outside Tonbridge in Kent. I can still remember the thrill of seeing Lady's-slipper in Yorkshire, long before it was so heavily guarded by wardens – sadly a necessary precaution – and finding, while feverishly swatting at a cloud of vicious horse-flies, the tiny green Bog Orchid in the New Forest. Then there have been the rare occasions when I have found orchids by the thousand where I had expected just a handful; orchids colouring the Sussex downland in a pink or mauve haze as far as the eye could see. Magic moments indeed!

Bog Orchids.

The purpose of this book is simple: to help people to make the most of their own magic moments with orchids. Its aim is to enable the orchid enthusiast, whether a beginner or an expert, to identify all the species, sub-species and varieties of Britain and Ireland's orchids they encounter. The text emphasises the differences between similar species, and is based on the very latest information. Identifying orchids can be immensely rewarding, enabling the observer to uncover further details of their fascinating lives. With this in mind, the book also contains sections on the life-cycle of orchids, their propensity for hybridisation, the habitats they occupy, and the potential for species new to Britain to spread here from abroad.

Given the length of time that orchids have been studied, it is immensely exciting to see that we are entering a new, and sometimes revolutionary, era in our understanding of them. Our perception of what constitutes a species, and how we apply this in a practical sense to the protection and conservation of our orchids, is likely to change rapidly. The chapter *Conservation in action* (*pages 166–172*) covers some of the ongoing studies and projects. We are extremely fortunate to live in a time when the emphasis on orchid conservation is placed firmly on encouraging people to enjoy, with respect, these magnificent plants in their natural habitat, rather than shrouding their locations in secrecy for fear that they will be damaged or removed.

Whilst it is relatively easy to find and study some species, many others remain highly endangered. This calls for active conservation and inevitably for the control of access by the orchid enthusiast if we are not to destroy the very things we love. Yet all is not doom and gloom and recent years have seen a heartening improvement in the status of a number of our rarest orchids. However, a great deal remains to be done if our descendants are to continue to enjoy what is truly a national treasure.

David Lang

9

An introduction to orchids

WHAT IS AN ORCHID?

I feel sure that I am not alone in having a plant pointed out to me by an enthusiastic naturalist with the question, "What orchid is this?", only to have to explain that it is not an orchid at all! So, what constitutes an orchid? Given the diverse nature of our relatively small orchid flora, and the manner in which some species can vary (see Bee Orchid *pages 150–153*, for example), the questioner should be excused and comforted.

Orchids belong to the Class of MONOCOTYLEDONS, in which the young plant emerging from the seed has a single juvenile leaf, known as a cotyledon. Within the Monocotyledons there are many other Families, which include plants such as Wild Arum, Autumn Squill, Bog Asphodel, various onions and garlics, rushes, sedges, grasses and lilies. Other flowering plants belong to the

Pyramidal Orchids.

Class of DICOTYLEDONS, where the emerging seedling has two leaves, typical examples being the seedlings of 'mustard-and-cress', which so many of us grew in class at primary school.

The Family ORCHIDACEAE are perennial plants with fleshy roots or tubers, and unstalked, undivided leaves which are often long and narrow, with parallel veins. There are, however, three species occurring in Britain – the Ghost, Bird's-nest and Coralroot Orchids – that have no proper leaves, these being reduced to scales sheathing the base of the stem. The flowers are carried in a spike or raceme, with a bract (a leaf-like structure) at the base of each flower stalk. The perianth segments (the sepals and petals) are carried above the tubular ovary (inferior ovary), which is divided into three compartments. The reproductive organs are carried on a specialised structure called the column. This combination of an inferior ovary and the presence of the specialised column serve to separate the orchids from the other Families in their Class of Monocotyledons.

Despite the apparent complexity of orchid flowers, they consist of six perianth segments divided into two whorls of three: the outer whorl of sepals and the inner whorl of petals. The lower petal is often large, prominent and complex, and is called the labellum or lip. In primitive orchids, the lip is positioned at the top of the flower, but in most of our orchids the flower has rotated 180° so that it comes to lie at the bottom. However, in one species, the Bog Orchid, the flower has rotated through 360°, and so adopts the 'primitive' position such that the flowers appear to be upside down.

In many species, the base of the lip is extended backwards as a pouch or spur, which may contain nectar. Its shape varies: in the butterfly-orchids, the spur is long and elegant; in the spotted-orchids it is slim and parallel-sided; whereas in the marsh-orchids it is fat and conical.

In the helleborines, the lip is divided into a basal, cup-shaped hypochile, which may secrete nectar, and a more or less triangular tip, the epichile, which is joined to the hypochile by a hinge. At the base of the epichile are two bumps or caruncles, the texture and colour of which are helpful in distinguishing the different species.

All the flowers carry both male and female reproductive organs on a structure called the column. The single stamen is divided into two club-shaped, pollen-bearing structures called pollinia (*singular* pollinium). Each mass of granular pollen is borne on a stalk called a caudicle, at the base of which is a sticky disc called a viscidium. The function of the viscidium is to adhere to any visiting insect, which will then carry it away to another flower so that cross-fertilisation can occur. There are three stigmata, the central sterile stigma forming the beak-like rostellum, with a fertile stigma on either side. In many species, the rostellum acts like a shelf, separating the pollinia from the stigma and thus preventing self-pollination. The two uppermost petals may form a protective hood over the reproductive organs.

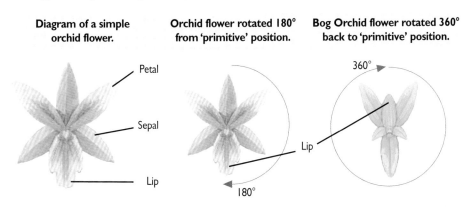

Diagram of a simple orchid flower.

Orchid flower rotated 180° from 'primitive' position.

Bog Orchid flower rotated 360° back to 'primitive' position.

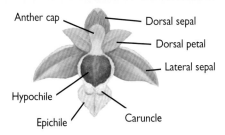

Frontal view of a typical helleborine flower.

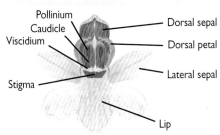

Frontal view of a typical orchid flower.

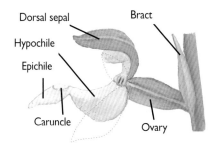

Lateral view of a typical helleborine flower.
(dorsal petal and lateral sepal removed to show lip).

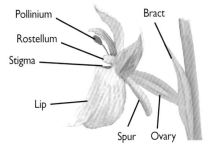

Lateral view of a typical orchid flower.

With this knowledge, take a closer look at the photograph of Autumn Squill below. Although the leaves are long and narrow, and the flowers are in a spike, each flower has six stamens arranged in a ring, and the ovary lies above the petals. The same is true of Bog Asphodel. Since the Bird's-nest Orchid lacks proper leaves, the brown colour of the whole flower spike can lead to confusion with the broomrapes – parasitic plants also lacking green chlorophyll. The tubular structure of the broomrape flowers, having an upper and a lower lip plus four stamens, should soon clarify the confusion. However, it is worth remembering that orchids are well known for producing abnormally shaped flowers, so that even the expert can be excused the occasional 'double take'!

Autumn Squill   Bog Asphodel   Knapweed Broomrape

GERMINATION AND GROWTH

Orchid seeds are very small, 0·1–0·25 mm long, and therefore carry little in the way of food reserves for the developing embryo. Not only must the site where the seed falls have ideal conditions of light, moisture and warmth, but the tiny plant which germinates must become infected immediately with a mycorrhizal fungus from the soil if it is to survive. Noel Bernard (1874–1911) first described this phenomenon, whereby the fungus initially acts like a parasite and attacks the orchid. The plant then checks it, breaking down the fungal cells, from which it derives the soil nutrients which it was incapable of obtaining for itself. According to the season of the year, either the orchid or the fungus will dominate, a process which is neither true parasitism nor symbiosis (two organisms co-existing for their mutual benefit).

As they mature, some orchid species will throw off the fungal infection and synthesize their own food, whilst others, such as the helleborines, are partially dependant upon their mycorrhizal fungus throughout their lives. Most orchids rely upon photosynthesis to make the bulk of their food, using the green pigment chlorophyll to fix energy from sunlight. The Bird's-nest Orchid, which has no green leaves and therefore no chlorophyll, is entirely saprophytic, deriving all its nutrients from the breakdown of organic material in the soil through a mass of fleshy roots heavily infected with mycorrhizal fungus.

When the orchid seed germinates, it forms a peg-like structure called a protocorm, which has a bud at one end and tiny rootlets. In time, fibrous roots and the first leaf are produced, at which stage the protocorm withers away. The process is very slow, more leaves and roots being formed each year until the plant reaches maturity and can flower. Early Spider-orchids can reach maturity in three years, the spotted-orchids and marsh-orchids in five or six years, while Burnt Orchids may take more than 15 years to reach the flowering stage for the first time.

Orchids are perennial, and during the winter die back to an underground tuber or root system, from which fresh leaves arise each spring. Bee Orchids form their new leaves in autumn, so that by the time the plants flower the leaves are often scorched and tattered. Autumn Lady's-tresses also forms autumn leaf rosettes but these have totally withered by flowering time, so that there are no leaves at the base of the current flowering stem. The sterile rosette of leaves alongside the flower will produce next year's bloom.

Many orchids are monocarpic – that is they flower once and then die – being entirely reliant upon seed production for future generations. Other species will flower repeatedly over a decade or more, although not necessarily every year. Yet others, such as the butterfly-orchids, will persist underground for years until conditions above ground become suitable - such as increased light following the removal of trees or scrub - when they will suddenly emerge and flower in large numbers.

A number of orchids are capable of multiplying by vegetative means. Some achieve this by growing two tubers instead of one, giving rise to the formation of clumps of individual plants. Musk Orchids develop new tubers on the end of stolons or runners, while Common Twayblade produces satellite plants from buds on a branching root system, so that the individuals appear to grow in lines radiating from the parent plant.

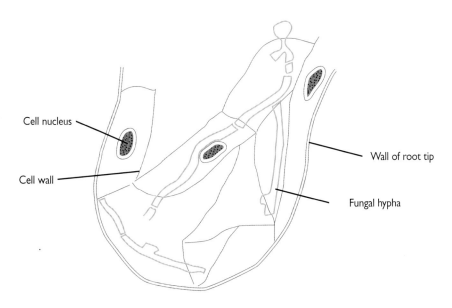

Orchid root tip showing mycorrhizal fungus (stained).

REPRODUCTION AND POLLINATION

The mechanism by which the pollinia become attached to the insect visitor has intrigued botanists from the time of Charles Darwin. Each club-shaped pollinium is borne on a long stalk, the caudicle, at the base of which is a sticky disc, the viscidium. A simple experiment can be made with the Early-purple Orchid, using a pencil point in place of the visiting insect's head. Insert the pencil point carefully into a flower, down into the spur. On withdrawing the pencil the two pollinia will be seen stuck on either side of the point. Watch carefully. Within a minute the pollinia will swivel downwards and forwards, ensuring that in any subsequent visit to a flower they will contact the stigma, set below the rostellum. The lapse of time taken for the pollinia to move ensures that the insect will have moved on to a different plant, so that cross-fertilisation can occur.

Bee Orchid flower showing the pollinia.

Some orchids, such as the Fragrant Orchid and the two butterfly-orchids, store nectar in the spur to attract insects, which in turn will carry pollen to other flowers to effect pollination. Other orchids, such as the Fly Orchid and Early Spider-orchid, secrete pheromones to attract the male insect vector, which attempts to copulate with the flower and in so doing gets the pollinia stuck onto its head or thorax. The late Howard Jones was the first to photograph this phenomenon – called pseudocopulation – in the 1970s and took some brilliant images of the Digger Wasp attempting to mate with the Fly Orchid.

A bumblebee with pollinia stuck to its head, on a Green-winged Orchid.

Many of the helleborines are self-pollinating. They do not secrete nectar in any quantity, and the rostellum is poorly developed, so that the pollen can fall directly onto the stigma – a procedure called autogamy. This can even occur before the flowers open, as recorded in the Bird's-nest Orchid and Green-flowered Helleborine – a procedure called cleistogamy.

The Bee Orchid appears to be designed to attract insect pollinators by mimicry, but this seldom happens. In nearly every case the caudicles shrink, dragging the pollinia out of their protective pouches, whence they swing downwards under their own weight to land on the surface of the stigma.

The pollinia of Pyramidal Orchids are conjoined at the base of the caudicles onto a single, saddle-shaped

A Digger Wasp 'mating' with a Fly Orchid flower.

viscidium. When the visiting insect, in this case a bee or a butterfly, inserts its proboscis into the spur in search of nectar, the viscidium is detached and clamps tightly around the proboscis. Within a very short time the pollinia swivel downward and outwards, perfectly positioned to hit the laterally placed stigmatic surfaces. Insects can sometimes be seen with several sets of pollinia stuck on their heads or probosces, resisting all attempts to dislodge them.

In the Common Twayblade, the pollen masses are very fragile and crumbly, set in a sticky mass which explodes when touched by small insects, thus allowing the pollen to fall directly onto the stigma.

Scent is an important attractant for insects. Both the butterfly-orchids are night-scented, an adaptation designed to attract the night-flying moths which act as pollinators. The scent of the Early-purple Orchid is initially sweet, but as soon as the flowers have been pollinated it changes to that of tom-cat's urine, presumably acting as a signal to potential insect visitors not to waste their time!

Data on the insect pollinators of our native orchids are, in many cases, rather sparse, presenting an opportunity for amateur observers to make a real contribution to our understanding of this process. However, obtaining photographs of a quality sufficiently high to permit accurate identification of the visiting insect is quite another matter! The mere fact that an insect is seen visiting an orchid does not mean that it is acting as a pollinator – it must be seen to remove pollinia if its role in the pollination process is to be confirmed.

Flies of the genus *Scathophaga* visiting a Burnt Orchid.

A Marsh Fritillary butterfly on Northern Marsh-orchid.

A bee (*Andrena nigroaena*) on an Early Spider-orchid.

A hoverfly on Dark-red Helleborine.

The crab spider *Misumena vatia* lurking on Southern Marsh-orchid spike – pollinators beware!

15

HYBRIDISATION

When we see garden flowers described as 'hybrids', we understand that they are the result of crossing two different types which may, or may not, be closely related. The same is true of our wild orchids. Most hybrids result in the wild from the crossing of plants that are closely related, but of different species. In the book *Hybridization and the flora of the British Isles* published in 1975, edited by Dr. C. A. Stace, a species is defined as "*a unit of practical value, visually recognisable and of evolutionary significance. Morphological and genetical data should be used in its recognition.*" Such hybrids between two different species within the same genus are termed 'interspecific'. Rarely, hybrids may result from plants belonging to different genera – 'intergeneric hybrids'.

The first generation offspring are called the F1 generation. These may in turn cross with either parent, a process called 'introgression', giving rise to a population showing a bewildering array of characteristics intermediate between the F1 hybrid and the parents. These 'hybrid swarms' are not uncommon where the spotted-orchids and marsh-orchids grow together and individual plants can be impossible to identify with certainty in the field. This situation can be made even more confusing if one of the parents dies out, perhaps as a consequence of environmental change, leaving the hybrid swarm with the other parent.

In a book published in 1951, V. S. Summerhayes described a hybrid between Common Spotted-orchid and Fragrant Orchid. The former has a pouch-like structure, known as a bursicle, around the pollinia, whereas Fragrant Orchid has none. The hybrid showed flowers with bursicles, partly formed bursicles and none at all – and all on the same flower spike!

Fly × Bee Orchid hybrid.

Early × Northern Marsh-orchid hybrid.

Hybrids between species will not occur if the populations are separated by too great a distance, or flower at very different times of the year. There are, however, other factors which may act to prevent the production of hybrids even where the parents grow close together. For example, pollen incompatibility may cause the pollen tube to die before it can reach the ovary, or the embryo produced may die before it can mature.

Hybrids can exhibit a paradoxical range of fertility. Hybrids between the closely related Common and Heath Spotted-orchids are highly sterile, whereas hybrids between unrelated species or even different genera can be fully fertile. In other cases, the F1 generation can be self-sterile (F1×F1 = sterile), but can reproduce by introgression.

In a paper published in 1923, Cockayne listed three criteria which had to be satisfied before it could be assumed that the plant under investigation was in fact a hybrid:
– it should have characteristics of both parents;
– both parents should grow nearby; and
– if the hybrid is fertile, there should be a separation of types in succeeding generations.

Satisfying all of Cockayne's criteria is not always straightforward. For example, whilst the hybrid between Fly and Bee Orchids clearly relates to both parents in appearance and is found at sites where the two species grow close together, the hybrid between Early and Northern Marsh-orchids bears little resemblance to either parent (see photographs opposite). In this case, though, the site where it occurs is very remote and the two species grow side-by-side. Genetic analysis of the plants has recently been undertaken and the identity of the parents confirmed.

Just to make matters more difficult for the inexperienced botanist, there will always be a considerable variation in both colour and markings within any large population of a single species. Just look at the range of colours sometimes found amongst a Green-winged Orchid colony or the variation in patterning on the flowers and leaves within a colony of Common Spotted-orchids. It is, therefore, important to beware of jumping to the conclusion that you have found a hybrid when you come across an unusual plant!.

A complete list of the hybrids recorded in Britain and Ireland is included on page 160; with photographs of some examples.

Green-winged Orchid colour forms.

Orchid habitats

A habitat is essentially a place where a plant or animal lives. In this book, the term is used to describe a distinctive community of plants. Some knowledge of Britain and Ireland's habitats is very useful finding orchids, since although some species are found in a range of places, many are 'habitat specific' – occurring in one, or a small number of habitats. Orchids can live in a wide range of habitats, from woodlands to grasslands, and from sea-level to our highest mountains. In Britain and Ireland, the different plant communities that make up our habitats, are largely formed as a result of the different soils and the underlying rock type on which they grow. Soils derived from, or overlying, alkaline or basic rocks such as chalk or limestone, or wetlands receiving water from those soils, such as alkaline fen, support a rich variety of orchids. Heathlands, moorlands and acid bogs support only a few species of orchid which can flourish in conditions of low pH.

Climatic conditions of temperature and rainfall also have a profound influence on the nature of the habitat. For example, the chalk grasslands of south-east England are very different from the limestone grasslands of Durness and Sutherland. They can be separated by an imaginary line from Durham, through Derbyshire to the Mendips, and skirting the Welsh coast. This line separates the relatively warm and dry climate of southern Britain from the cooler, wetter climate further north.

This section of the book provides an introduction to the habitats that are home to our native orchids highlighting the orchid species which can typically be found in each.

GRASSLAND

CHALK AND LIMESTONE GRASSLAND

Downland is a type of pasture typical of southern England, which has generally developed on steep chalk or limestone slopes with extensive sheep grazing. The tradition of using the river valleys in the winter to gain an 'early bite' for livestock, and the chalk ridges for summer grazing has led to a species-rich turf which often includes a range of orchids. Whilst much has fallen under the plough – particularly with the UK's drive to become self-sufficient in food during the Second World War – superb stretches of downland still remain on the South Downs in Sussex, in Hampshire, Wiltshire, Dorset, the Chilterns and the Cotswolds. The short turf is rich in flowers and is colourful, comprising the yellows of Common Bird's-foot-trefoil and hawkweeds, the blues of scabious and milkworts and the pink of the dwarf Squinancywort. The orchid flora is often very diverse, including Early and Late Spider-orchids, Bee, Frog, Musk, Fragrant and Pyramidal Orchids, Greater and Lesser Butterfly-orchids, and Early-purple, Green-winged and Burnt Orchids. The

Chalk grassland on the South Downs, East Sussex.

latter are virtually restricted to ancient, undisturbed pasture, except for one site at Martin Down in Wiltshire, where they have spread onto an area ploughed during the Second World War.

The Breckland of Norfolk and Suffolk was probably cleared of trees in the Neolithic period. There, the soil is a fine, acid sand overlying chalk, and supports a number of rare flowers such as Spiked Speedwell, Maiden Pink and Spanish Catchfly. Early Spider-orchid was found there in 1991 – the first time it had been recorded in Suffolk since 1793.

Breckland grassland.

The limestone grasslands of northern England, in the Dales of Yorkshire and Derbyshire, are particularly species-rich. Burnt Orchid reaches its northernmost site in Wharfedale, while the magnesian limestone grassland of east Durham carries most of the species found in southern England, with the addition of Dark-red Helleborine. In Scotland, there are small areas of superb limestone grassland in Glen Clova, Angus; and at Inchnadamph and Durness, Highland. Here, the Fragrant Orchid occurs mainly as the sub-species *borealis*, together with Frog Orchid, Small-white Orchid and Dark-red Helleborine.

Coastal calcareous grassland, Purbeck, Dorset.

COASTAL LIMESTONE GRASSLAND

This very special habitat exists in a number of sites on the west coast of Britain, from the Gower peninsula in south Wales, northwards to the Ayrshire coast. Bounded by sea cliffs on one side and arable fields inland, it is never extensive. The finest example is, without doubt, found on the Dorset coast over the Purbeck limestone between Swanage and Lulworth, where pride of place must go to the Early Spider-orchid, which numbers in tens of thousands in a good year.

NEUTRAL GRASSLAND

Many of Britain's traditional pastures and meadows were established on land which was neither strongly acidic nor calcareous. These traditionally-managed 'neutral' grasslands are the main habitat in Britain for Green-winged Orchid. Although examples remain in many counties, this habitat has suffered more than most from the intensification of agriculture in recent decades. Activities such as ploughing, reseeding, cutting early for silage and the application of high levels of artificial fertilisers all have a detrimental effect on orchids, as well as other sensitive plants. It is, therefore, not surprising that the Green-winged Orchid has declined more than any other species of orchid in recent years.

Neutral grassland with Green-winged Orchids, Marden, Kent.

MACHAIR

Machair habitat is peculiar to the west coast of the Hebridean Islands, apart from a few isolated pockets situated on the west coast of mainland Scotland, and on the western seaboard of Donegal to Kerry and on the Mullet peninsula in Co. Mayo in Ireland. The finest stretches occur on the Outer Hebrides, such as North and South Uist, Benbecula, Barra and Tiree. Machair is found on the western shores of the islands and comprises flat grazing areas overlying wind-blown shell sand, inland from the coastal sand dunes. In the past these areas provided improved grazing on 'township' commons under a system called 'souming'. They were grazed by moderate numbers of cattle, although the number sometimes increased during the winter months. After the early 1800s, the grazing became dominated by sheep. Machair grasslands have been influenced by arable cultivation since Viking times. Later on, there was a rotation of crops, oats and potatoes, then reverting to grass, with seaweed being spread as a manure. In recent years this practice has declined as the use of artificial fertilisers has increased, with grants only awarded on production of an empty plastic bag. Great care had to be taken to prevent overgrazing and the erosion of the thin 'skin' of plant growth, since the strong winds experienced on the coasts that are exposed to the Atlantic gales could result in catastrophic 'blow-outs', and the subsequent destruction of the precious grazing land.

Machair on South Uist.

The flowering of the machair in early June is breathtaking – a virtual carpet of flowers – with buttercups, daisies, Bloody Crane's-bill, Sea Stork's-bill, Common Bird's-foot-trefoil, Harebell, Lady's-bedstraw and Rue-leaved Saxifrage. The orchid flora is also fantastic, with millions of spikes of the dwarf sub-species *hebridensis* of Common Spotted-orchid and both the sub-species *incarnata* and the striking, brick-red *coccinea* of Early Marsh-orchid, as well as Lesser Butterfly-orchid, Frog Orchid and Common Twayblade.

DUNE SLACKS

Dune slacks are part of a constantly evolving habitat. On the seaward side a fringe of sand forms on the debris found along the tide-line. This gradually builds up and is colonised by a few species of plants which are able to tolerate these exposed conditions. Once the sand dune has built up, it is then colonised by Marram Grass. A little way inland, away from the sea, further dunes form which are rich in calcareous shell debris. Wind action and rain combine to create flat zones between the dunes which are fractionally above the level of the water table. These areas are known as dune slacks and may contain transient pools of water.

Dune slacks at Ynyslas, north Wales.

This uncommon habitat is characterised by extensive areas of Creeping Willow, which further stabilises the sand against erosion by wind, and a ground cover of Red Fescue, daisies, thyme, Fairy Flax, Water Mint, Marsh Pennywort and Variegated Horsetail. Plants that are more often associated with chalk downland, such as Lady's-bedstraw and Yellow-wort, mingle with typically coastal plants such as Sea Holly, Sea Spurge and Portland Spurge.

Dune slacks are incredibly rich in orchids, both in quantity and in interesting species, depending upon where the dunes are sited. They occur from Braunton Burrows in north Devon, along the south Wales coast at Kenfig and Oxwich, on the north Wales coast at Ynyslas, Morfa Dyffryn and Morfa Harlech, Newborough Warren on Anglesey and Ainsdale on the coast of Lancashire. In Scotland, they occur on the east coast at Culbin Sands in Morayshire and Tentsmuir in Fife. In Ireland this habitat can be found all around the coastline (*e.g.* Magilligan Point, Co. Derry; Tramore Dunes, Co. Waterford; Killala Bay, Co. Mayo; and Bull Island, Co. Dublin).

Marsh-orchids can be abundant in dune slacks and form spectacular displays, particularly the brick-red sub-species *coccinea* of the Early Marsh-orchid. Helleborines are also well represented, with Marsh, Green-flowered and Dune Helleborine occurring in Wales and Lancashire. Most important are the populations of the broad-leaved variety *ovata* of Fen Orchid in south Wales, where colonies can be extensive. However, this species is highly sensitive to environmental change and only thrives in newly-formed dune slacks which are scarcely above the level of the water table. It therefore relies upon a succession of new dune slacks being formed, into which they can seed and spread.

In addition to their marsh-orchids, the dune slacks on the east coast of Scotland contain Lesser Twayblade, growing in moss under Heather, and Creeping Lady's-tresses. Both species occur where the ground is drier, often under planted coniferous trees. Dune slacks in North Uist are the habitat for the rare sub-species *scotica* of the Western Marsh-orchid.

LIMESTONE PAVEMENT

The almost lunar appearance of limestone pavement is unforgettable. At first glance, the landscape resembles porridge, with grey, continuous cover. However, on closer inspection it will be seen to be composed of flat blocks (or clints) separated by deep cuts or fissures (known as grykes). Small areas can occur wherever there is exposed Carboniferous limestone, but the most spectacular stretches of limestone pavement in England are at Gait Barrows in Lancashire and Souther Scales below Ingleborough in Yorkshire. Smaller areas exist from south Cumbria up to Durness in Sutherland. All are fascinating, with a rich flora often sheltering deep in the grykes where it is warm and sheltered. Here it is possible to find Bloody Crane's-bill, Angular Solomon's-seal and the poisonous Baneberry, as well as orchids including Common Twayblade, Early-purple, Fly and Small-white Orchid as well as Dark-red Helleborine.

The finest limestone pavement of all is known as The Burren, which is situated in Co. Clare on the west coast of Ireland. In this area, a number of different plant groups combine to form unique communities at sea level, and include species such as Mountain Avens, Spring Gentian and Dense-flowered Orchid – this latter orchid is now restricted to this area. Amongst the stretches of limestone are small seasonal lakes, or turloughs, along the edges of which flourish Fly Orchids, Lesser Butterfly-orchids, the rare sub-species *cruenta* of Early Marsh-orchid and the white-flowered sub-species *okellyi* of Common Spotted-orchid.

Limestone pavement on The Burren, Co. Clare.

LIMESTONE CLIFFS

Limestone cliffs rarely support large orchid populations, as they are exposed and liable to erosion. Nevertheless, they can serve as places of refuge for plants from the teeth of grazing sheep. Good examples can be found in the Avon Gorge in Somerset, Dovedale in Derbyshire and in many sites in North and West Yorkshire, such as Malham Cove, Gordale Scar, Arncliffe, Kilnsey Crag and Pen-y-ghent. The Carboniferous limestone cliffs of the Gower peninsula in south

Limestone cliffs at Dovedale, Derbyshire.

Wales are superb for plants, as are the cliffs of Inchnadamph and Durness in west Sutherland. Dark-red Helleborine is particularly prevalent on these northern cliffs, while Frog Orchid and the northern sub-species *borealis* of Fragrant Orchid can be found on the grassy slopes at their feet.

MARSH

Marshes have often been formed as the result of human activity. From Roman times onwards, land has been reclaimed from the sea by walling off tidal mudflats. These then become colonised by reeds as the salinity decreases, and finally dry out and become used for grazing land. A similar process has led to marshland forming along the banks of slow-flowing rivers in flood-plains. Many of these marshes have been drained in recent centuries, but they still exist in north Kent and Essex along the Thames, the Pevensey Levels in East Sussex, the Lymington Marshes in Hampshire, the Somerset Levels, along the river valleys of Suffolk, Norfolk and Cambridgeshire, and particularly along the Lincolnshire coast.

Marsh-orchids can be found along the edges of wet marshes, where they are not out-competed by Common Reeds. Early, Southern, Northern and Narrow-leaved Marsh-orchids are all recorded, with smaller numbers of Greater and Lesser Butterfly-orchids and Heath Spotted-orchid. Coastal marshes can also hold extensive populations of Marsh Helleborine.

Marsh at Warnborough Green, Hampshire.

FEN

Fen is formed in low-lying areas which become waterlogged, and on the edges of lakes and rivers where the water recedes sufficiently in the spring to permit plant growth. If there is a high level of calcium carbonate in the water, and a consequently high pH, then fen will develop with a rich flora. The chemical properties of surface water are highly variable, and this in turn will lead to a wide variation in fen characteristics, with varying proportions of reeds, rushes, sedges and grasses, interspersed with ferns and horsetails.

Fen is a fragile and greatly threatened habitat, with small areas still remaining in Cambridgeshire, Norfolk, Suffolk, Anglesey and the Somerset Levels. In AD 1637 it is estimated that fenland in East Anglia covered 3,380 square kilometres.

Redgrave and Lopham Fen, Suffolk.

Drainage here started in earnest in 1630, with the aid of the famous Dutch engineer Vermuyden. The area that remains today is barely ten square kilometres in extent and is very fragmented. The Norfolk Broads formed as the result of extensive medieval peat cuttings and subsequent inundation, but even this area has been much altered by drainage and pollution, with the subsequent loss of fen habitat.

Fen contains both interesting and very rare orchids. Early, Southern and Narrow-leaved Marsh-orchids all grow in fenland, as does the tall fen sub-species *densiflora* of Fragrant Orchid and Marsh Helleborine. However, the rarest species, and the most important of all in terms of conservation, is the Fen Orchid in its true fenland form. This is now reduced to a handful of plants in three sites in east Norfolk. This species is afforded a high priority for conservation action under the UK Biodiversity Action Plan, and is the subject of a recovery plan (see *page 168*).

BOG

Bogs can form wherever water becomes trapped and the ground surface remains consistently saturated. The water involved may be primarily rainwater or predominantly ground water and the types of bog which result are significantly different in their importance for orchids. Although both types of bog are poor in minerals and nutrients, and characterised by acid-loving plants such as *Sphagnum* mosses and sundews, they differ in particular in the movement of water through the developing peat.

Valley bog and wet flush on Crane's Moor, New Forest, Hampshire.

Bogs which obtain their water entirely from rainfall occur mainly in the west and north of Great Britain and Ireland where the rainfall is high, and they form on gently sloping or flat terrain, usually over an acid substrate. They can be divided into two types:

♦ **RAISED BOG** which forms on a flat underlying surface, frequently as an infill of glacial lakes, and has a gently dome-shaped profile, with peat deepest at the centre.

♦ **BLANKET BOG** which forms in areas with such a high rainfall that moss, and hence peat, can develop over more sloping terrain. The vegetation literally smothers gently-sloping uplands in a blanket, following the land contours. It is this type of bog which covers huge areas of the 'flow country' in east Sutherland and Caithness.

Bogs that are more influenced by ground water also form in very gently-sloping river valleys. They are especially frequent in places such as the New Forest, although small examples can be found almost anywhere in Great Britain and Ireland, and are much less dependent upon a high rainfall. These bogs usually have greater water flows and as a result are less nutrient deficient and better oxygenated. Consequently, the number of orchids occurring in these types of bog tends to be greater than in raised or blanket bogs.

Bogs are composed of mosses, predominantly *Sphagnum* species, with sundews and creeping plants such as Dewberry, Crowberry and Cranberry. In the more mature, drier, areas plants such as Bilberry, Ling, Heather and Dwarf Birch also occur. Since the environment is acidic, orchids are not widespread, although species such as Heath Spotted-orchid, Lesser Butterfly-orchid and Lesser Twayblade are found. Bogs are, of course, the habitat of the rare Bog Orchid which flourishes in the saturated moss. Important areas for bogs include the New Forest in Hampshire, on Dartmoor and Exmoor, throughout Wales and on Anglesey, the Cheshire and Shropshire meres and mosses, the Solway and Duddon mosses of Cumbria, Thorne and Hatfield moor in Yorkshire, and all of upland northern England and Scotland. They are very extensive in central and northern Ireland.

ACID HEATHLAND AND MOORLAND

Heathland and moorland are mostly comprised of shrubby species including heathers and gorses. Whilst lowland heathland characterises generally dry areas, moorland occurs at higher altitude and in wetter districts. Trees tend to be sparse, chiefly scattered Pine and Birch, with a ground cover including shrubs such as European and Dwarf Gorse, Heather, Ling and Bilberry. They originated following the clearance of woodland with fire by early human settlers in the Neolithic and Early Bronze Ages. Moorland covers large areas of Scotland, Wales, Ireland and the north of England, with similarly extensive areas on Exmoor and Dartmoor in the south-west.

Moorland, Rannoch Moor, Highland.

Lowland heathland characterises areas of southern and central England. Relatively small pockets remain in the Ashdown Forest in East Sussex, in West Sussex, the New Forest of Hampshire, parts of the Breckland in East Anglia, the Dorset heaths, in Devon and on the Gower in south Wales. The ancient heathlands of the Lizard peninsula in Cornwall lie over outcrops of serpentine rock, and host a number of rare plants, including Cornish Heath. Further north, there are the 'Coversands' of Lincolnshire and Humberside.

Orchids are not often present in large numbers on heathland, Heath Spotted-orchid being the most widespread and plentiful species, with marsh-orchids in damp areas. In the northern half of Britain, sub-species *pulchella* of Early Marsh-orchid and Northern Marsh-orchid are the most common. Lesser Butterfly-orchid occurs sporadically and Lesser Twayblade is not uncommon, growing in *Sphagnum* mosses under the heather.

LOW MONTANE

Low montane comprises a mosaic of many different types of habitat. It occurs in Wales, northern England, Scotland and Ireland up to an altitude of 500 m. It is an area of high rainfall, but the habitat lacks the extremes of exposure and cold experienced in truly mountainous areas. The countryside comprises a patchwork of unimproved pasture and small hay meadows with extensive areas of moorland and exposed rock. Stream valleys have birch as the dominant tree species, whilst lakes and lochans may be bordered by bog.

Orchids may not be numerous, but some less common and fascinating species can be found in these areas. Heath Spotted-orchid is once more the most common species, with Northern Marsh-orchid occurring in the damper areas. Lesser Butterfly-orchid, Small-white Orchid and the northern sub-species *borealis* of Fragrant Orchid grow in the old pasture areas, with Lesser Twayblade in the rocky parts and even

Low montane habitat at Tir Stent, Dolgellau, Gwynedd.

Bog Orchid on the edge of flushes and stony runnels. In north-west Scotland, Lapland Marsh-orchid grows in damp hill flushes, with the rare Irish Lady's-tresses on the edge of hill lochs and rivers which are inundated in the winter.

BROAD-LEAVED WOODLAND

Broad-leaved woodland is primarily a feature of lowland Britain, becoming less extensive further north. The dominant species of trees changes with latitude, resulting in a wide variation of woodland types. Each type of woodland favours different orchid species which have differing preferences for light and shade, depth of leaf litter and competition from shrubs and other ground flora.

Beech woodlands support the most exciting orchid flora. Mature Beech woodland with a typically light ground cover of Dog's Mercury can be found along the North and South Downs, in Hampshire, Wiltshire and Dorset, the Chilterns and the western end of the Cotswolds. White Helleborine and the rarer Narrow-leaved Helleborine can occur in considerable numbers, with the very rare Red Helleborine found in favoured sites. Bird's-nest Orchid also occurs, often with the unrelated but similar-looking Yellow Bird's-nest. Rare inhabitants include Lady Orchid, Narrow-lipped Helleborine and Ghost Orchid, the latter restricted entirely to mature Beech woodland within which there is a deep layer of litter.

Early-purple Orchids under Ash coppice at Kings Wood, Heath and Reach National Nature Reserve, Bedfordshire.

Woodland composed of Beech mixed with birch, Field Maple and whitebeam, with a ground cover including Bramble, Lords-and-Ladies and Wood Anemone, is also widespread along the North and South Downs, the New Forest and the Chilterns. Additional orchid species that occur here include both Broad-leaved and Violet Helleborine, the latter tolerating more shade, Early-purple Orchid, Common Twayblade, Green-flowered Helleborine, Fly Orchid and the two splendid relatives, Lady Orchid and Military Orchid.

Coppicing is a form of woodland management practised mainly in the south of England. Woodland composed of Hazel, Hornbeam and Sweet Chestnut is periodically cut down to ground level, producing broad-based 'stools' from which multiple, tall, straight branches grow, ideal for use in hedge-laying or as hop-poles. Early-purple Orchids, Common Twayblade, Fly and both Greater and Lesser Butterfly-orchids all flourish, particularly under Hazel and Hornbeam, as does Lady Orchid in Kent. As the trees grow and the canopy thickens orchid numbers tend to decrease, but, in the first couple of years after fresh coppicing, they can be spectacular.

In the west and north, from Dartmoor to Sutherland, but especially in mid- and north Wales and the Lake District, the dominant broad-leaved woodland consists of Sessile Oak mixed with Downy Birch, Rowan and Holly. The understorey is predominantly Bilberry and Heather and sometimes includes Creeping Lady's-tresses, but this is a generally poor habitat for orchids. Upland woodlands containing Ash and Hazel mixed with Rowan and Downy Birch are far more open in character with plentiful Dog's Mercury and flowers such as Solomon's-seal and Wood Crane's-bill. Orchids are few in number, but this is the habitat for the lovely Lady's-slipper where there is underlying limestone.

In north Yorkshire, Cumbria, south and north-east Scotland there is woodland composed of Bay Willow growing over a peaty soil, with a healthy growth of sedges such as Bottle Sedge. This is one habitat where Coralroot Orchid may be found.

PINE WOODLAND

Ancient pine forest, composed of Scot's Pine, is now entirely restricted to small remnants of the Caledonian Forest of Scotland, such as that in Glen Feshie, Highland. Trees are spaced well apart, with a dense ground cover of Heather, Ling, Bilberry and Crowberry. In places there can be shelter and a dense carpet of moss, with fascinating flowers such as Twin-flower, Common, Round-leaved and One-flowered Wintergreens.

Caledonian Pine Forest, Loch Maree, Highland.

Orchids such as Creeping Lady's-tresses flourish and their root systems run through the moss carpet, with Lesser Twayblade growing in *Sphagnum* under the Heather and Coralroot Orchid in slightly drier sites.

Planted conifers, especially plantations of closely-ranked Sitka Spruce, are valueless as orchid habitat, but some areas such as the Culbin Forest in Morayshire and Tentsmuir Forest in Fife have matured over the years and become superb orchid habitat.

ROAD VERGES, LAWNS AND CHURCHYARDS

Whilst most human activity spells doom for orchids, we have managed, despite ourselves, to create habitat which is highly supportive of the more opportunistic orchid species.

Road verges – provided that they are subject to sympathetic management and not regularly mown – can support stunning populations of Common Spotted-orchids, Early-purple Orchids and Pyramidal Orchids. Bee Orchids seem almost to relish the disturbance, and will appear in impressive numbers on recently graded roadsides. Their numbers then decrease over succeeding years. Experimental work is currently being carried out involving the scarification of certain motorway verges to see if Bee Orchid numbers respond positively.

Road verge at Amberstone, East Sussex.

Lawns, tennis-courts and churchyards can provide equally productive orchid habitat, with Common Spotted-orchids, Early-purple Orchid, Green-winged Orchid and Autumn Lady's-tresses all gracing suitably managed grass. Indeed, Autumn Lady's-tresses benefits from a well-maintained, mown sward, the leaf rosette being so flat that the mower blades do no harm.

FLY-ASH TIPS AND LAGOONS

Of all the habitats which appear to be unpromising for orchids, fly-ash tips and lagoons must seem among the worst. Each year, 10 million tons of ash is produced from coal-burning power stations. Much is used in the construction industry but the rest is disposed of as mounds or as lagoons. Initially barren, the first plants to appear are species of goosefoots and salt-marsh grasses, plants that are well able to cope with the high level of mineral salts in the substrate. Over many years there is a gradual sequence of development, with birch and willow appearing and then, after some 10–20 years, orchids starting to colonise, weathering having reduced the ash to a base-rich 'soil'. Common Spotted-orchid, Early and Southern Marsh-orchid are the first to appear, often in impressive numbers, including swarms of hybrids. Bee Orchid has also been recorded, as has Marsh Helleborine on very mature sites. Unfortunately, some of the orchid sites have to be 'restored', since this was part of the original planning consent. Access to these sites is inevitably restricted for safety reasons.

Particularly interesting orchid sites exist in the Cheshunt gravelpit complex in the Lee Valley in Hertfordshire, at the Carmarthen Bay wind energy centre, at the old Wilford power station site in Nottinghamshire, at Wakefield and Wigan power stations in Yorkshire, and at other sites such as Rye House in Hertfordshire, Meaford in Staffordshire, Fiddlers Ferry in Lancashire and Elland in West Yorkshire.

Southern Marsh-orchids at a post-industrial site, Canvey Island, Essex.

An introduction to the species

This section provides a summary of the key features of the orchids that are native to Britain and Ireland. It provides an introduction to the identification of the species by grouping together those of similar appearance. Each species is illustrated with a close-up photograph of a typical individual floret and the text is cross-referenced to the relevant plates(s) which show the whole plant. It is important to be aware that there can be considerable variation in the colour and/or shape of the flowers, and that hybrids sometimes occur (see *page 160*).

SINGLE (OR 2) VERY LARGE FLOWERS WITH AN INFLATED LIP

Genus: *Cypripedium*

Lady's-slipper
Cypripedium calceolus   *Page 42*

PLANT: 30–50 cm.
LEAVES: broad, clasping, strongly furrowed.
FLOWER: very large; petals and sepals erect, red-brown;
           lip yellow, slipper-shaped.

FLOWERS UNSTALKED, NOT OPENING WIDE; LIP DIVIDED INTO TWO HALVES

Genus: *Cephalanthera*

White Helleborine
Cephalanthera damasonium   *Page 44*

PLANT: up to 60 cm.
LEAVES: narrow, ribbed, in 2 ranks.
FLOWER: ivory-white; 5 yellow ridges on upper surface of lip.

Narrow-leaved Helleborine
Cephalanthera longifolia   *Page 46*

PLANT: up to 160 cm.
LEAVES: long and pointed, in 2 ranks.
FLOWER: held away from stem; pure white;
           3 orange ridges on upper surface of lip.

Red Helleborine
Cephalanthera rubra   *Page 48*

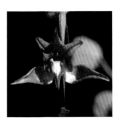

PLANT: up to 60 cm.
LEAVES: dark green, pointed and ridged.
FLOWER: pink, covered in glandular hairs;
           5-7 orange ridges on upper surface of lip.

Genus: *Epipactis*

Marsh Helleborine
Epipactis palustris   *Page 50*

PLANT: 20–60 cm.
LEAVES: pointed, ridged and folded.
FLOWER: pinkish; outer half of lip white, frilled with
yellow plate across base.

Dark-red Helleborine
Epipactis atrorubens   *Page 52*

PLANT: 15–30 cm.
LEAVES: in 2 ranks; broad, ridged and folded.
FLOWER: brick-red; outer half of lip recurved with
3 rough bumps at base.

Violet Helleborine
Epipactis purpurata   *Page 54*

PLANT: up to 60 cm.
LEAVES: pointed; grey-green, may be violet-tinged.
FLOWER: pink or greenish-pink; outer half of lip recurved with
2 smooth, pink bumps at base.

Broad-leaved Helleborine
Epipactis helleborine   *Page 56*

PLANT: robust, up to 90 cm.
LEAVES: arranged in a spiral; very broad, ribbed, clasping stem.
FLOWER: green to reddish; outer half of lip recurved with
2 rough, brown bumps at base.

Young's Helleborine
Epipactis helleborine var. *youngiana*   *Page 58*

PLANT: robust, up to 60 cm.
LEAVES: in 2 ranks; broad, wavy-edged; yellow-green.
FLOWER: bell-shaped, drooping; outer half of lip pinkish with
green centre and 2 rough bumps at base.

Narrow-lipped Helleborine
Epipactis leptochila   *Page 60*

PLANT: 15–60 cm.
LEAVES: in 2 ranks; broad and floppy.
FLOWER: greenish; outer half of lip long, not recurved, pointed
with 2 pink bumps at base.

31

Dune Helleborine

Epipactis dunensis  *Page 62*

PLANT: up to 60 cm.

LEAVES: in 2 ranks; yellow-green; stiff and clasping.

FLOWER: greenish-pink; outer half of lip pink, tip recurved with bumps at base ill-defined.

'Lindisfarne' Helleborine

Epipactis sancta  *Page 64*

PLANT: up to 60 cm.

LEAVES: yellow-green, broad and stiff, in two rows up the stem.

FLOWER: yellowish-green; lip whitish-green, with a green tip; narrow join between epichile and hypochile.

Green-flowered Helleborine

Epipactis phyllanthes  *Page 66*

PLANT: up to 40 cm.

LEAVES: smooth, blunt and clasping.

FLOWER: green; scarcely opening; lip small; ovary fat and pear-shaped.

PLANTS LACKING LEAVES AND GREEN CHLOROPHYLL

Genus: *Epipogium*

Ghost Orchid

Epipogium aphyllum  *Page 68*

PLANT: 5–25 cm.

LEAVES: none.

FLOWER: pinkish-yellow; sepals and petals drooping, red-spotted; lip broad, pink with purple papillae on upper surface.

Genus: *Neottia*

Bird's-nest Orchid

Neottia nidus-avis *Page 70*

PLANT: stout, up to 50 cm.

LEAVES: none.

FLOWER: honey-brown; lip divided into 2 broad, spreading lobes.

Genus: *Corallorhiza*

Coralroot Orchid

Corallorhiza trifida  *Page 88*

PLANT: 6–28 cm.

LEAVES: none.

FLOWER: sepals yellow, tipped brown; lip white with crimson spots.

Two basal leaves section.

TWO BASAL LEAVES; FLOWERS SMALL WITH FORKED LIP

Genus: *Listera*

Common Twayblade
Listera ovata   *Page 72*

PLANT: up to 75 cm.
LEAVES: very broad and ribbed.
FLOWER: green; lip forked into 2 long lobes.

Lesser Twayblade
Listera cordata   *Page 74*

PLANT: 3–10 cm.
LEAVES: heart-shaped; bright green.
FLOWER: tiny; reddish-brown; lip forked into 2 thin lobes.

WHITE FLOWERS SET IN AN OBVIOUS SPIRAL UP THE STEM

Genus: *Spiranthes*

Autumn Lady's-tresses
Spiranthes spiralis   *Page 76*

PLANT: 5–15 cm.
LEAVES: none on current flowering spike.
FLOWER: trumpet-shaped; lip gutter-shaped and frilled.

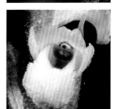

Summer Lady's-tresses   (EXTINCT)
Spiranthes aestivalis   *Page 78*

PLANT: 10–40 cm.
LEAVES: yellow-green; narrow and pointed.
FLOWER: narrow, trumpet-shaped; lip a broad gutter.

Irish Lady's-tresses
Spiranthes romanzoffiana   *Page 80*

PLANT: 10–30 cm.
LEAVES: yellow-green; narrow, grass-like.
FLOWER: fat, tubular, covered in short hairs; lip green-veined.

Genus: *Goodyera*

Creeping Lady's-tresses
Goodyera repens   *Page 82*

PLANT: 8–35 cm.
LEAVES: stalked, pointed oval, net-veined.
FLOWER: small, very hairy; tending to face one direction.

Genus: *Liparis*

Fen Orchid
Liparis loeselii   *Page 84*

PLANT: 5–20 cm.
LEAVES: 'fen form' narrow, pointed and shiny;
          'dune form' broad and clasping.
FLOWER: yellow-green with narrow sepals;
          lip spear-shaped, folded into a gutter.

Genus: *Hammarbya*

Bog Orchid
Hammarbya paludosa   *Page 86*

PLANT: tiny, 3–12 cm.
LEAVES: 2, small, rounded; bulbils on rim.
FLOWER: tiny, green; lip green-striped, pointing upwards.

Genus: *Herminium*

Musk Orchid
Herminium monorchis   *Page 90*

PLANT: 5–15 cm.
LEAVES: small; strap-shaped; yellow-green.
FLOWER: tiny; bell-shaped; sepals and petals pointed; lip 3-lobed.

Genus: *Platanthera*

Greater Butterfly-orchid
Platanthera chlorantha   *Page 92*

PLANT: 26–60 cm.
LEAVES: shiny, broad and elliptical.
FLOWER: white with green flush; lip long; spur very long (2·5 cm),
          down-curved; pollinia, set wide apart, converge upwards.

Lesser Butterfly-orchid
Platanthera bifolia   *Page 94*

PLANT: 15–55 cm.
LEAVES: shiny, broad and elliptical.
FLOWER: white with green flush; lip long; spur very long
          and fairly straight; pollinia parallel, set close together.

34

Genus: *Anacamptis*

Pyramidal Orchid
Anacamptis pyramidalis   *Page 96*

PLANT: 10–60 cm.
LEAVES: numerous, narrow and pointed.
FLOWER: spike pyramidal; spur long; lip with two erect plates at base.

Genus: *Gymnadenia*

Fragrant Orchid
Gymnadenia conopsea   *Pages 100–103*

PLANT: 10–40 cm.
LEAVES: numerous, narrow, pointed and folded.
FLOWER: spur long and down-curved.

Genus: *Pseudorchis*

Small-white Orchid
Pseudorchis albida   *Page 98*

PLANT: 10–40 cm.
LEAVES: basal leaves broad and flat; stem leaves pointed.
FLOWER: small, cup-shaped and greenish-white; lip 3-lobed with longer central section; spur thick, conical, down-curved.

Genus: *Neotinea*

Dense-flowered Orchid
Neotinea maculata   *Page 128*

PLANT: 10–40 cm.
LEAVES: basal leaves broad, bluish-green; may have lines of tiny red dots.
FLOWER: small, white or rarely pink; scarcely opening; central lobe of lip forked.

Genus: *Coeloglossum*

Frog Orchid
Coeloglossum viride   *Page 104*

PLANT: 5–15 cm.
LEAVES: blunt, strap-shaped.
FLOWER: yellow-green or brown; lip paler with tip three-lobed.

Genus: *Dactylorhiza*

Common Spotted-orchid
Dactylorhiza fuchsii   *Pages 106–109*

PLANT: up to 70 cm.

LEAVES: numerous, narrow pointed and usually spotted, sometimes heavily-marked.

FLOWER: pink or pale lilac, marked with dark spots and lines; strongly 3-lobed.

Heath Spotted-orchid
Dactylorhiza maculata ssp. *ericetorum*   *Page 110*

PLANT: 10–40 cm.

LEAVES: numerous, pointed; lightly marked with small spots.

FLOWER: pink or pale lilac, marked with reddish spots and lines; lip broad, shallowly 3-lobed with short central lobe.

Genus: *Dactylorhiza*

Early Marsh-orchid
Dactylorhiza incarnata   *Pages 112–117*

PLANT: 10–35 cm.

LEAVES: narrow, yellow-green; unspotted (except ssp. *cruenta*) with hooded tips.

FLOWER: creamy-white, pink, purple or brick red depending on sub-species; lip shallowly 3-lobed, sides strongly bent back, marked with double loop and spots in red.

Southern Marsh-orchid
Dactylorhiza praetermissa   *Page 118*

PLANT: robust, to 70 cm.

LEAVES: numerous; broad, flat and unhooded; unspotted.

FLOWER: deep lilac or magenta; lip flat, scarcely 3-lobed with marks that do not form loops.

Northern Marsh-orchid
Dactylorhiza purpurella   *Page 120*

PLANT: 10–35 cm.

LEAVES: broad; glaucous-green.

FLOWER: deep lilac or mauve; lip diamond-shaped, heavily marked with dark flecks.

Western Marsh-orchid
Dactylorhiza majalis   *Page 122*

PLANT: 15–35 cm.

LEAVES: numerous, broad, flat and unspotted except for ssp. *scotica* which has very heavily-marked leaves.

FLOWER: mauve; lip broad, 3-lobed with rounded central lobe, well-marked with spots and lines.

Narrow-leaved Marsh-orchid
Dactylorhiza traunsteineri   *Page 124*

PLANT: 20–45 cm.

LEAVES: narrow and grass-like; unspotted.

FLOWER: pale or dark mauve; sepals and petals long, elegant; lip 3-lobed with long central lobe.

Lapland Marsh-orchid
Dactylorhiza lapponica   *Page 126*

PLANT: 6–24 cm.

LEAVES: apple-green, heavily marked with violet-brown spots and blotches.

FLOWER: dark purple; lip and sepals heavily-marked with dark flecks.

FLOWERS PURPLE WITH UPTURNED SPURS

Genus: *Orchis*

Early-purple Orchid
Orchis mascula   *Page 130*

PLANT: 10–60 cm.

LEAVES: numerous, blunt and shiny; may be heavily-spotted.

FLOWER: purple; 3-lobed lip with sides slightly bent back, centre marked with dark spots; spur stout, blunt.

Green-winged Orchid
Orchis morio   *Page 132*

PLANT: 5–15 (rarely 40) cm.

LEAVES: numerous and blunt; unspotted.

FLOWER: predominantly purple (white or pink occasional); centre of lip pale with dark flecks; sides of lip bent back; spur stout, tip inflated; lateral sepals marked with dark green parallel lines.

Genus: *Orchis*

Burnt Orchid
Orchis ustulata   *Page 134*

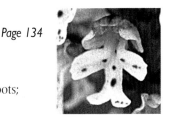

PLANT: 5–10 cm.
LEAVES: broad, channelled and strongly-veined.
FLOWER: hood deep red-brown; lip white with crimson spots; lobes all blunt.

Lady Orchid
Orchis purpurea   *Page 136*

PLANT: robust, up to 100 cm.
LEAVES: broad, blunt and shiny.
FLOWER: hood dark; lip shaped like lady in a crinoline dress; white with purple spots formed of tiny hairs.

Military Orchid
Orchis militaris   *Page 138*

PLANT: robust, 20–60 cm.
LEAVES: broad, blunt and shiny.
FLOWER: lilac rose; hood pale, dark-striped within; lip pinkish, narrow with 2 'arms' and 2 broader 'legs', marked with lines of purple spots formed of tiny hairs.

Monkey Orchid
Orchis simia   *Page 140*

PLANT: 10–30 cm.
LEAVES: blunt, glossy and keeled.
FLOWER: spike opens from the top downwards; shaped like a little monkey with 4 limbs and a tail; 'paws' darker violet-purple.

Genus: *Aceras*

Man Orchid
Aceras anthropophorum   *Page 142*

PLANT: 15–40 cm.
LEAVES: blue-green, blunt and veined.
FLOWER: yellow-green or foxy-red; hood tight; lip narrow, divided into 2 two narrow 'arms' and 2 narrow 'legs'.

Genus: *Himantoglossum*

Lizard Orchid
Himantoglossum hircinum   *Page 144*

PLANT: robust, 25–70 cm.
LEAVES: broad, though withered by flowering time.
FLOWER: grey-green; hood small, lined with brown dots; lip with
         2 crinkly, brown side-lobes and very long, twisted
         tongue-like central lobe, the base marked with crimson
         spots said to resemble a lizard.

PLANTS WITH COLOURFUL FLOWERS RESEMBLING INSECTS

Genus: *Ophrys*

Fly Orchid
Ophrys insectifera   *Page 146*

PLANT: 15–60 cm.
LEAVES: blunt, very shiny and floppy.
FLOWER: sepals yellow-green; upper petals like 'antennae' of a fly;
         lip mahogany-brown, marked in the middle with an
         iridescent blue band.

Early Spider-orchid
Ophrys sphegodes   *Page 148*

PLANT: 5–20 cm.
LEAVES: grey-green, broad and veined.
FLOWER: sepals yellow and erect; lip convex, brown and
         furry, marked with a distinctive smooth 'H'.

Bee Orchid
Ophrys apifera   *Pages 150–153*

PLANT: 15–50 cm.
LEAVES: grey-green; strap-shaped, tips often look scorched.
FLOWER: sepals pink and erect; lip resembles a brown and
         yellow furry bee. There are 9 distinct forms of flower.

Late Spider-orchid
Ophrys fuciflora   *Page 154*

PLANT: 15–55 cm.
LEAVES: strap-shaped and well-veined.
FLOWER: sepals pink and erect; upper petals triangular,
         orange-coloured and hairy; lip broad and furry,
         brown and yellow with yellow appendage at tip.

This table provides a summary of the main flowering period of each orchid.

	APR	MAY	JUN	JUL	AUG	SEP	OCT
Lady's-slipper		■	■				
White Helleborine		■	■				
Narrow-leaved Helleborine		■	■	■			
Red Helleborine				■			
Marsh Helleborine				■	■	■	
Dark-red Helleborine			■	■			
Violet Helleborine					■	■	
Broad-leaved Helleborine				■	■	■	
Narrow-lipped Helleborine			■	■	■		
Dune Helleborine			■	■	■		
'Lindisfarne' Helleborine				■	■		
Green-flowered Helleborine				■	■		
Ghost Orchid			■	■	■	■	■
Bird's-nest Orchid	■	■	■				
Common Twayblade	■	■	■	■			
Lesser Twayblade		■	■	■			
Autumn Lady's-tresses					■	■	
Summer Lady's-tresses				■	■		
Irish Lady's-tresses					■		
Creeping Lady's-tresses				■	■	■	
Fen Orchid			■	■			
Bog Orchid				■	■	■	
Coralroot Orchid		■	■	■			
Musk Orchid			■	■			
Greater Butterfly-orchid		■	■	■			
Lesser Butterfly-orchid		■	■				
Pyramidal Orchid			■	■	■		
Small-white Orchid		■	■	■			
Fragrant Orchid		■	■	■	■		
Frog Orchid			■	■	■	■	
Common Spotted-orchid		■	■	■	■		
Heath Spotted-orchid		■	■	■	■		
Early Marsh-orchid		■	■	■			
Southern Marsh-orchid			■	■			
Northern Marsh-orchid		■	■	■			
Western Marsh-orchid		■	■				
Narrow-leaved Marsh-orchid		■	■				
Lapland Marsh-orchid			■	■			
Dense-flowered Orchid		■					
Early-purple Orchid	■	■	■				
Green-winged Orchid	■	■	■				
Burnt Orchid		■	■	■	■	■	
Lady Orchid	■	■	■				
Military Orchid		■					
Monkey Orchid		■	■				
Man Orchid		■	■				
Lizard Orchid			■	■			
Fly Orchid	■	■	■				
Early Spider-orchid	■	■					
Bee Orchid			■	■			
Late Spider-orchid				■			

Introduction to the Species accounts

The species accounts are grouped in this section as follows:

- Pages 42–155: the 51 species which are known to have occurred naturally in Britain and/or Ireland.
- Pages 156–159: the nine species which have occurred but are of uncertain or doubtful provenance.

The text is cross-referenced to other parts of the book as appropriate, including the section on pages 30–39, which includes a photograph of a typical floret for each species. The format used for the species accounts is summarised on this page:

English name
Scientific name
previous or possible future scientific name

IDENTIFICATION
A concise description of the plant, detailing the key identification features.

CONFUSING SPECIES
A list of the species with which confusion is possible, cross-referenced to the relevant species account(s).

HYBRIDS
A list of the known hybrids.

TAXONOMIC STATUS
Notes on taxonomy (if appropriate).

HABITAT
A summary of the habitat preferences.

POLLINATION
Details of the means of pollination and known pollinators.

CONSERVATION
Notes on conservation action and threats.

Wherever possible, English names are used for other species mentioned in the text. The scientific names for these species are given on page 179.

ABUNDANCE IN BRITAIN & IRELAND
Locally abundant

MEASUREMENTS
The species' vital statistics.

Height:	up to 60 cm
No. of flowers:	up to 16

FLOWERING PERIOD
When to go and look for the species.

FLOWERING PERIOD
Early May to end of June

DISTRIBUTION MAP
Purple shading indicates the extent of the species' known distribution.

DISTRIBUTION
A summary of the species' distribution, with notes on some of the best locations and, where appropriate, specific sites for the species.

DISTRIBUTION
Relatively common in south-east England on the North and South Downs and the Chilterns, west to Somerset, Devon and south-east Wales. Absent from Scotland and Ireland. Many sites have been lost in recent years, but the species is capable of extensive colonisation of recently planted Beech woods.

STATUS
Where appropriate, a summary is given of the status and legislative protection afforded to the species (see page 164).

CRITICALLY ENDANGERED
EC Habs Dir. Annexes II & IV
W&C Act Schedule 8
W(NI) Order Schedule 8
UK BAP Priority Species

THE PLATES
Shows the plant and, where appropriate, a close-up of the flower-head and/or an individual floret.

Lady's-slipper
Cypripedium calceolus

IDENTIFICATION
A robust plant, 30–50 cm tall, with up to five broad, strongly furrowed and veined, alternate, yellow-green leaves, which sheath the stem. The bract is large and erect, standing up like a hood behind the flower. Most plants carry a single flower, rarely two. The sepals and petals are a deep reddish-brown. The lateral sepals, 3–5 cm long, are slightly twisted. The two lower sepals are conjoined, so that the broad sepals and petals form a cross behind the big, yellow, slipper-shaped lip, which is 2–3 cm long. The inside of the lip is marked with lines of orange dots. The opening of the pouch-like lip is partly blocked by the large, tongue-shaped staminode which also bears orange dots.

CONFUSING SPECIES
None.

HYBRIDS
None known.

HABITAT
Steep, grassy slopes at the foot of limestone 'scars', also in light woodland with Ash, Hazel and stunted oak.

POLLINATION
Bees of the genus *Andrena* act as pollinators in Europe, and are present where the orchid grows in Yorkshire. However, they are only attracted to groups of flowers and tend to ignore single plants. The bee enters the 'slipper' easily, but can only get out by pushing between the side of the pouch and the staminode, receiving a dusting of pollen in the process.

CONSERVATION
Over-collection for specimens and gardens led to the virtual extinction of the Lady's-slipper. Current problems include damage by slugs, snails, voles and Rabbits. Public access is strictly controlled. See the *Conservation in action* section on *page 167*.

Very rare

Height: 30–50 cm
No. of flowers: usually 1

FLOWERING PERIOD
Late May to early June

DISTRIBUTION
Reduced to one native site in Yorkshire. Seed collected there was grown under laboratory conditions and, since 1989, seedlings have been re-introduced to sixteen classic sites where it had grown in the past. For further details, see the *Conservation in action* section on *page 167.*

CRITICALLY ENDANGERED
EC Habs Dir. Annexes II & IV
W&C Act Schedule 8
UK BAP Priority Species

White Helleborine
Cephalanthera damasonium
previously: *Cephalanthera latifolia*

IDENTIFICATION
Robust, up to 60 cm tall. Leaves oval, strongly ribbed, in two rows up the stem, merging into leaf-like bracts longer than the ovary. Up to 16 ivory-white flowers carried upright, parallel to the stem. Flowers do not open widely, concealing the blunt yellow lip. The epichile of the lip bears five parallel, dark yellow ridges on the upper surface, the outermost two sometimes poorly formed. These seem attractive to insects and are often nibbled away. The ovary is broader near the tip, deeply grooved and not twisted. Flowers with double lips and double columns can occur, as can plants with white stems and leaves.

CONFUSING SPECIES
Narrow-leaved Helleborine (*page 46*) has elegant, long pointed leaves, pure white flowers standing out from the stem, a lip with three ridges on the epichile, and a twisted ovary.

HYBRIDS
The hybrid with Narrow-leaved Helleborine (see photograph on *page 161*) is intermediate in character but rare, having been found only twice in Sussex and Hampshire.

HABITAT
Woodland on chalk or limestone with little ground cover, especially Beech woods where it can occur in considerable numbers. Occasionally found on open downland.

POLLINATION
Most flowers are efficiently self-pollinated, although pollination by the female solitary bee *Andrena florea* has been recorded. Mature plants develop in eight years from seed, but may not flower for another two to three years.

CONSERVATION
Although the species is still plentiful in suitable habitats, many populations have been lost through inappropriate woodland clearance.

Locally abundant

Height: up to 60 cm
No. of flowers: up to 16

FLOWERING PERIOD
Early May to end of June

DISTRIBUTION
Relatively common in south-east England on the North and South Downs and the Chilterns, west to Somerset, Devon and south-east Wales. Absent from Scotland and Ireland. Many sites have been lost in recent years, but the species is capable of colonising recently planted Beech woodlands.

Narrow-leaved Helleborine

Cephalanthera longifolia

previously: *Cephalanthera ensifolia*

Widespread but rare

Height: up to 160cm

No. of flowers: up to 40

FLOWERING PERIOD

Early May to 1st week July

IDENTIFICATION

Robust. Up to 160 cm tall in favoured sites, more often 25 cm. Leaves long, pointed and elegant, longest in mid-stem. One of our most beautiful orchids, with up to 40 pure white flowers held well out from the stem, which has a blind shoot at its apex. The petals and sepals are long and pointed, tending to arch outwards revealing the lip which bears three parallel orange ridges on the epichile. Ovary slender, parallel-sided and spirally twisted through 180°. Plants in exposed sites have much shorter stems and fewer flowers.

CONFUSING SPECIES

White Helleborine (*page 44*) has broader, blunt leaves, ivory white flowers, a lip with five ridges and an untwisted, fat ovary.

HYBRIDS

The hybrid with White Helleborine (see photograph on *page 161*) is rare, as the two species seldom grow near each other.

HABITAT

In the southern half of England it occurs in open glades in woodlands, chiefly Beech on chalk or mixed Ash and Oak on limestone. In these well-lit sites it often grows underneath taller competing vegetation. In the Wyre Forest in Hereford it grows on acid soils in Sessile Oak woodland with Bilberry. Sites in Scotland lie over limestone or calcareous schist. In Ireland it grows on The Burren, Co. Clare in cracks between the limestone pavement, while near the sea in Mayo it grows in wind-blown calcareous sand overlying peat.

POLLINATION

Female solitary bees of the species *Lasioglossum smeathmannellum* and *L. fulvicornis* have been recorded as pollinators, but seed-set is poor since the rostellum prevents self-pollination.

CONSERVATION

A declining and threatened species, due in the main to habitat destruction. Now part of English Nature's Species Recovery Programme, and Plantlife International's 'Back from the Brink' project, funded by English Nature. In Wales it has been lost from eight of its 14 known sites. See the *Conservation in action* section on *page 169*.

DISTRIBUTION

Declining in sites and numbers everywhere probably due to changes in woodland management and the planting of conifers. Substantial populations remain in Hampshire. Still extant in five sites in Wales near the sea, in Cumbria, and widely-spread up the west coast of Scotland from Arran to Sutherland, although in small numbers. Occurs at a few sites in the west of Ireland, where the plants are small and have few flowers

Red Helleborine
Cephalanthera rubra

Very rare

Height: up to 60 cm
No. of flowers: up to 6

IDENTIFICATION
An unmistakable helleborine, with up to six large, bright pink flowers which in bud resemble a small freesia. Up to 60 cm tall, but usually much smaller, with rather dark green, shortish leaves and narrow pointed bracts longer than the narrow, spirally twisted ovary. Petals and sepals long and pointed, arching back to expose the pointed pink lip, which has a pale yellow centre. There are five to seven orange ridges on the epichile. The outer surfaces of all the floral parts are covered with tiny glandular hairs.

CONFUSING SPECIES
None.

HYBRIDS
None known in Britain, but the hybrid with Narrow-leaved Helleborine has been recorded in Europe.

HABITAT
Well drained deciduous woodland, chiefly Beech, on chalk or limestone. Often to be found on steep slopes. Not a large plant, competing poorly with other vegetation, but capable of remaining in a vegetative state for many years.

POLLINATION
The male mason bee *Osmia caerulescens* and a small solitary bee, possibly *Chelostoma fuliginosa*, have been recorded visiting flowers, as have small hoverflies and the Small Skipper butterfly.

CONSERVATION
Despite careful management, it is declining in two of its present known locations. Seed-set has rarely been observed, probably because of the scarcity of the necessary insect pollinators in Britain. See the *Conservation in action* section on *page 166*.

FLOWERING PERIOD
Late June to late July

DISTRIBUTION
Now known from only three sites in Britain: in Gloucestershire, where it has been known for some years; in Buckinghamshire, where it was discovered in 1955, and in Hampshire, where it was discovered in 1986. Previously recorded from three other sites in Gloucestershire, from Kent, and doubtfully from three sites in West Sussex, from Berkshire Hertfordshire and Somerset. Clearance of old woodland could result in its rediscovery dormant plants responding to the increased light

CRITICALLY ENDANGERED
W&C Act Schedule 8

Marsh Helleborine
Epipactis palustris

Uncommon

Height: up to 60 cm
No. of flowers: up to 20

IDENTIFICATION

A charming species, whose resemblance to a tiny *Cymbidium* satisfies the popular concept of an orchid flower. 20–60 cm tall, with an extensive creeping root system. Leaves numerous, pointed and folded, three to five strongly marked veins, leaf bases sometimes tinged violet. Flower spike one-sided with up to 20 flowers. Ovary pear-shaped, untwisted. Sepals pointed, purplish-brown, petals white with pink base. Lip divided into cup-shaped hypochile marked with parallel red veins and broad white epichile with a white frilled edge and a crinkly yellow plate across the base. Var. *ochroleuca* **och** lacks the red-brown colours, having greenish-yellow sepals, and white petals and lip; it occurs widely.

CONFUSING SPECIES

Its preferred habitat and flamboyant flowers make confusion with other helleborines unlikely.

HYBRIDS

None known in Britain.

HABITAT

Calcareous fens, marshes, wet meadows and dune slacks where shell sand supplies the necessary lime. One of the orchids found in recent years to colonise fly-ash pools. Known from two sites on chalk hills in Bedfordshire and north Wiltshire. Prefers sites which are seasonally inundated by water.

POLLINATION

Subject to much argument, depending on the geographical area recorded. Honeybees, a small black wasp *Psen palustris*, hoverflies, and a cantharid beetle, the bloodsucker *Rhagonychus fulva* have all been implicated. Ants are important, their feeding activities disrupting the pollen masses which then fall onto the stigma. Insect pollination is effective, but within a colony vegetative multiplication by aerial shoots which develop on the extensive rhizomes is more important.

CONSERVATION

In most areas this is a decreasing species, especially in southern England, where recent dry summers have led to further losses. Most sites were lost prior to 1930 following the drainage of wet areas.

FLOWERING PERIOD
Early July to early September

DISTRIBUTION
Most populations occur in coastal areas of East Anglia, south and south-west England, Wales Lancashire and across Ireland. Rare in Scotland on the west coast, on Coll, Colonsay and Islay and one recently discovered (1983) site in the Central Highlands

W(NI) Order Schedule 8

och

Dark-red Helleborine

Epipactis atrorubens

previously: *Epipactis atropurpurea* and *Epipactis rubiginosa*

IDENTIFICATION

15–30 cm tall, with a softly hairy stem, especially in the upper part. Leaves in two opposite rows, folded, strongly veined and rough on both surfaces. Upper leaves longer, and all may be red-tinged at their bases. Up to 20 flowers, usually a deep wine-red colour, rarely cream-coloured (Wester Ross). Sepals usually longer than the petals, pointed and incurved. There is great variation; some flowers are small and cup-shaped, others have long, elegant, spreading sepals. The hypochile is usually greenish within, the red margined epichile small, reflexed, with three wrinkled red bosses at its base sometimes extending as a v-shaped ridge to the tip of the epichile. Anther cap bright yellow, making a vivid contrast. Ovary pear-shaped, downy.

CONFUSING SPECIES

Broad-leaved Helleborine (*page 56*) with dark red flowers, but thay can be differentiated by the distinctive lip structure.

HYBRIDS

Hydridises with Broad-leaved Helleborine in north Wales, northern England and the north of Scotland where the species co-exist. Both are pollinated by wasps.

HABITAT

Restricted to exposed limestone cliffs, limestone pavement and the faces of limestone quarries. It is a striking sight growing out of clefts in the cliff face or in the deep grikes between the blocks of the limestone pavement. In the Burren in County Clare, Ireland it also occurs in *Dryas* (Mountain Avens) heath growing over limestone.

POLLINATION

Insects appear attracted by scent. Wasps, bumblebees and honeybees may all act as pollinators. The hoverfly *Scaeva pyrastri* has been photographed with the tips of its antennae just protruding through a mass of pollen glued to its head. Small beetles have also been recorded as visitors. Seed-set is efficient.

CONSERVATION

Damage can occur where the orchids grow in limestone quarries which are being worked. Grazing by sheep can also be a problem.

Height: up to 30 cm
No. of flowers: up to 20

FLOWERING PERIOD
June to early August

DISTRIBUTION
Found in Yorkshire, Lancashire and Durham, North Wales, in isolated colonies in East Perth and Morayshire, and then northwards up the west coast of Scotland from West Ross to the far north coast of Sutherland. On the east coast of Skye. In Ireland it is a great feature of The Burren limestone of County Clare and Galway.

Nationally Scarce

Violet Helleborine

Epipactis purpurata

previously: *Epipactis sessilifolia* and *Epipactis violacea*

Local in south, south-east and central England

Height: up to 60 cm
No. of flowers: up to 100

FLOWERING PERIOD
August and September

IDENTIFICATION

Up to 60 cm tall, with a tendency to grow in clumps of as many as 20 spikes, but usually shorter and with fewer spikes. The leaves are narrow, well-ribbed and a distinctive grey-green colour. Leaf bases and leaf-sheaths may be suffused with a violet colour. Flowers in a one-sided, tightly-packed spike, with long bracts giving it a 'leafy' appearance. Sepals and upper petals pointed, green and spreading. The lip has a pale brown lined hypochile, the epichile recurved, often pink-tinged, with two smooth, bright pink bosses at the base. Ovary rough, with short hairs.

Plants totally lacking in chlorophyll **ach** have been recorded recently in West Sussex, Surrey and Wiltshire. The leaves are a luminous pinkish-violet and the flowers are white. In a gloomy wood they almost seem to glow. The term used for this form is achlorophyllous.

CONFUSING SPECIES

Narrow-lipped (*page 60*) and particularly Broad-leaved Helleborine (*page 56*). Peak flowering period is some two weeks later than for these two species, but their total flowering periods overlap by as much as a month. The best distinguishing features are the narrow, dark leaves and the bosses on the base of the epichile.

HYBRIDS

Hybrids with Broad-leaved Helleborine have been recorded.

HABITAT

Lowland deciduous woodland, often heavily shaded particularly with Beech, on chalk soils and 'clay-with-flints'. Also in Hazel and Hornbeam coppice on sandy or clay soils. Requires more shade than the Broad-leaved Helleborine can tolerate. An amazingly tough plant, capable of pushing up through several inches of newly-laid tarmacadam.

POLLINATION

Mainly by male Cuckoo Wasps and possibly by short-headed wasps *Paravespula* spp. The hoverfly *Episyrphus balteatus* has been recorded visiting flowers, and may remove pollen masses.

CONSERVATION

Loss of habitat has led to an overall decrease in the last 50 years.

DISTRIBUTION
Most plentiful in south-central and south-east England in Kent, Surrey and the Chilterns, also in Worcestershire. Recently discovered west to Dorset (1989) and Somerset (1987), and north as far as Shropshire (1987). May occur elsewhere but has been overlooked.

Broad-leaved Helleborine

Epipactis helleborine
previously: *Epipactis latifolia*

Height: up to 90 cm
No. of flowers: up to 100

FLOWERING PERIOD
Early July to early September

IDENTIFICATION
Robust and tall, up to 90 cm; can form small clumps. Leaves broad, strongly ribbed, arranged spirally up the stem. Up to 100 flowers borne in a one-sided spike. Ovary strongly ribbed and smooth. Sepals blunt, upper petals smaller and pinkish. Lip divided into a cup-shaped hypochile, dark red and sticky within, and a pinkish, wedge shaped epichile, the tip strongly reflexed. The base of the epichile bears two rough, brown bosses. Flower colour varies from greenish where plants grow in shade to deep reddish-brown in sunny sites. Chlorotic plants, where all parts are pale yellowish-green, have been reported widely.

CONFUSING SPECIES
All the helleborines except Marsh Helleborine (*page 50*). Look for the broad leaves, robust growth and the two diagnostic rough bosses on the base of the epichile in this species.

HYBRIDS
Hybrids with Violet, Dark-red and possibly Narrow-lipped Helleborines have been recorded where the species grow together.

TAXONOMIC STATUS
Young's Helleborine (*page 58*) was formerly considered to be a full species, but recent genetic research has suggested that it is part of the variation found in Broad-leaved Helleborine. As such it does not warrant species or even sub-species status, and probably is best regarded as a variety, the taxonomy we have followed here.

POLLINATION
Self-pollination is rare in Britain. The German Wasp and another wasp *Dolichovespula sylvestris* are the most important insect pollinators. They lap nectar stored in the hypochile, seeming to get very sleepy or drunk, and have even been seen falling out of the flowers. Ants have been recorded removing the entire pollinium.

CONSERVATION
No particular conservation concerns; capable of colonising new forestry plantations.

DISTRIBUTION
Widely distributed throughout England, Wales and central Scotland. In Ireland it is less common, scattered mainly in the north and west.

HABITAT
Mainly found on calcareous soils, but will tolerate slight acidity. Grows in broad-leaved and coniferous woodlands, especially on road and track verges where there is plenty of sunlight. Also on limestone cliffs and pavements, dune slacks and even in town gardens, such as in Glasgow where it is relatively common.

Young's Helleborine

Epipactis helleborine var. *youngiana*

previously: *Epipactis youngiana*

Rare

Height: up to 60 cm
No. of flowers: up to 30

FLOWERING PERIOD
July

IDENTIFICATION

When growing in full sun it can be robust, up to 60 cm tall, with four to seven narrow, wavy-edged leaves carried in two ranks up a solitary, slender stem which bears short hairs on the upper half. The leaves are yellowish and do not have well-marked veins. The flower spike is one-sided, with 12 (rarely up to 30) broadly bell-shaped, drooping flowers. The lateral sepals are long and curve outwards, the petals blunt and pink-edged. The lip is strongly reflexed, the hypochile spotted inside with purple and the heart-shaped epichile bearing two well-marked, rough bosses which are often confluent and may extend to the tip of the epichile. The epichile is usually pink with a green central zone. The stigma has three sharp, forwardly directed points, the central upper point being formed by the rostellum. This feature is diagnostic.

CONFUSING SPECIES

The yellowish leaves and the shape, colour and markings of the lip help to separate it from Broad-leaved (*page 56*), Narrow-lipped (*page 60*) and Green-flowered Helleborines (*page 66*).

HYBRIDS

Possible hybrids have been noted with Broad-leaved and Narrow-lipped Helleborines.

TAXONOMIC STATUS

Although once considered to be a full species, recent genetic research suggests it is a distinct and recognisable variety of Broad-leaved Helleborine. In south Tyne and in Wales it grows with Broad-leaved and Green-flowered Helleborines, while in Scotland it grows with Broad-leaved and Narrow-lipped Helleborines.

DISTRIBUTION
In England it is known from south Northumberland and east Yorkshire, in Wales from Glamorgan and in Scotland from Lanarkshire and Midlothian.

HABITAT

First identified in 1976 in oakwoods on a clay soil in south Tyne. A second population was found on river gravels heavily contaminated with zinc and lead, the site of an abandoned lead mine. There it grows under Alder, Sallow and birch, with planted pine trees, Spring Sandwort and Common Wintergreen. In Scotland it has been found on old coal-bings and spoil-heaps overgrown with oak, Ash and birch.

POLLINATION

Usually self-pollinated. The German Wasp has been observed visiting flowers, but has not been seen to remove pollinia. Ants visit the flowers to drink secretion from the hypochile.

CONSERVATION (See also *page 166*)

Two colonies have been lost as the result of woodland clearance.

ENDANGERED
W&C Act Schedule 8

Narrow-lipped Helleborine

Epipactis leptochila

previously: *Epipactis cleistogama*

Local

Height: up to 60 cm
No. of flowers: up to 25

FLOWERING PERIOD
Early June to mid-August

IDENTIFICATION

15–60 cm tall, frequently with multiple stems. The broad, yellow-green, floppy leaves grow in two ranks up the stem, the lower bracts being longer than the flowers. There are up to 25 pendulous flowers set all round the stem. The green sepals and petals are long, pointed and spreading. The hypochile of the lip is brown within. In the southern populations the epichile is extremely long, pointed and not reflexed. There are two poorly defined, smooth, pinkish bosses at the base of the epichile, separated by a deep V-notch formed in the outer rim of the epichile. In Scottish plants the epichile is shorter and is often reflexed. In south Tyne both types of lip can be found in the same population.

CONFUSING SPECIES

All *Epipactis* species except Marsh Helleborine (*page 50*). In southern populations of Narrow-lipped Helleborine, the long sepals and petals, and the long, straight lip, are the most helpful identification features.

HYBRIDS

Plants intermediate between this species and the Dune Helleborine have been recorded.

TAXONOMIC STATUS

See the section on Taxonomic Status under Dune Helleborine (*page 62*).

HABITAT

Found in two distinct habitats. Plants in southern England are strongly calcicolous, occurring in fairly dense Beech or Hornbeam woods on chalk; also in Ash and whitebeam scrub on limestone, where the shade is often dense. In the north of England and Scotland it is recorded under birch and Alder on zinc- and lead-polluted river gravels, and under regenerating oak, Ash and birch on coal-bings and spoil-heaps.

POLLINATION

Usually self-pollinated. In Northumberland the German Wasp has been seen removing pollinia.

CONSERVATION

Many woodland sites in south England have been lost as the result of clearance or the planting of conifers.

DISTRIBUTION
Woodland on chalk and limestone in central-southern and southern England; elsewhere, at inland sites only in Lincolnshire, Yorkshire, Northumberland, and in Scotland south of Glasgow. In 1979, a population of what appears to be this species was found growing at a site in south-east Co. Antrim, Northern Ireland, but the colony may subsequently have been destroyed as a result of the plantation being clear-felled.

Nationally Scarce

60

Dune Helleborine

Epipactis dunensis

previously: *Epipactis leptochila* var. *dunensis*

Rare

Height: up to 60 cm
No. of flowers: up to 30

FLOWERING PERIOD
Early June to mid-August

IDENTIFICATION

Up to 60 cm tall, leaves yellow-green, broad and stiff, in two rows up the stem. All the bracts are shorter than the flowers. Sepals and petals relatively short and blunt, resulting in a cup-shaped flower. Sepals and petals yellowish-green. Lip pinkish-white, with a green tip. The epichile is broader than long, with a recurved tip, especially as the flower matures. The bosses at the base of the epichile are poorly defined. Flowers may shrivel early in a dry season.

CONFUSING SPECIES
Narrow-lipped (*page 60*) and Broad-leaved Helleborines (*page 56*).

HYBRIDS
Plants intermediate between this species and Narrow-lipped Helleborine have been recorded.

TAXONOMIC STATUS
Recent research work on the allozymes and DNA of Narrow-lipped and Dune Helleborines seems to indicate that they are truly distinct. Plants from the south of England and continental Europe form one group and should be referred to as *Epipactis leptochila*, while those from coastal dune sites of north Wales and north-west England should be referred to as *Epipactis dunensis*. Plants from inland sites in Northumberland and Scotland may yet prove to constitute a third group. Some populations there contain plants apparently of both species, with intermediate forms to further complicate the picture. Furthermore, plants from Lindisfarne, once regarded as Dune Helleborine, have proven to be a distinct species – 'Lindisfarne' Helleborine (*page 64*).

DISTRIBUTION
Coastal dune sites in Anglesey and Lancashire. Inland sites in Northumberland, Cumberland, Lanarkshire, West- and Mid-Lothian.

HABITAT

Characteristically a plant of moist areas in coastal sand dunes, occasionally spreading into nearby conifer plantations. Also in zinc- and lead-polluted inland sites, coal-bings and spoil-heaps with a sparse overstorey of Ash, birch and Alder.

POLLINATION

Usually self-pollinated.

CONSERVATION

Although grazing by Rabbits in coastal sites helps to maintain the habitat, over-grazing can lead to habitat destruction.

'Lindisfarne' Helleborine

Epipactis sancta
previously: *Epipactis dunensis* p.p.

Rare

Height: up to 60 cm
No. of flowers: up to 30

FLOWERING PERIOD
mid-July to mid-August

IDENTIFICATION

The 'Lindisfarne' Helleborine can grow up to 60 cm tall, although it is usually shorter. The leaves are yellow-green, broad and stiff, and in two rows up the stem. The sepals and petals are yellowish-green, and the lip whitish green with a green tip. The epichile is broader than long, with a recurved tip, especially as the flower matures. The join between the epichile and the hypochile is narrow. The rostellum is elongated and although a viscidium may be present in some buds and young flowers it is very weak and disappears as the flower matures. In addition, the surface of the stigma is at right angles to the long axis of the ovary making the pollinia erect with bases touching the stigmatic surface, all features which help distinguish 'Lindisfarne' Helleborine from other closely-related species occuring in Britain and Ireland.

CONFUSING SPECIES
Dune (*page 62*), Narrow-lipped (*page 60*) and Broad-leaved Helleborines (*page 56*).

HYBRIDS
None recorded.

TAXONOMIC STATUS
Recent genetic research has shown this localised plant to be sufficiently both genetically and morphologically distinct from its close relatives, Dune and Narrow-lipped Helleborines, to merit species status in its own right. Taxonomically 'Lindisfarne' Helleborine was previously regarded (p.p.) as being part of the Dune Helleborine species.

POLLINATION
Usually self-pollinated.

CONSERVATION
The population of the 'Lindisfarne' Helleborine is small and restricted to a fragile dune habitat. At present, there are no specific conservation measures in place but as all the plants are within a National Nature Reserve they are protected by the associated legislation and afforded conservation priority.

DISTRIBUTION
A population of around 300 plants is confined to Lindisfarne National Nature Reserve, off the Northumberland coast.

HABITAT
Characteristically a plant of the coastal sand dunes of Lindisfarne NNR, occurring in a defined habitat zone lying between the higher, less stable dune tops and the lower, stabilised dune habitat consisting of dune slacks and willow carr.

Green-flowered Helleborine

Epipactis phyllanthes

previously: *Epipactis vectensis, Epipactis pendula* and *Epipactis cambrensis*

Widespread but uncommon

Height: up to 40 cm
No. of flowers: up to 20

FLOWERING PERIOD
Late June to end of July

IDENTIFICATION

A very variable helleborine. Woodland plants are often small, 10–40 cm tall, the lower stem leaves stiff, rounded and almost waxy in texture, with up to 16 stem leaves in two ranks. Most plants have only three or four leaves. Up to 20 flowers in a fairly dense, drooping spike, the green flowers looking disproportionately small on the fat, grooved, pear-shaped ovaries. The sepals and petals are green and pointed, often barely opening to reveal the small, greenish lip with reflexed epichile. In some flowers the hypochile is shallow and poorly differentiated. Plants growing in sand dunes tend to be more robust, with greenish-yellow, coarsely ribbed leaves, but like the plants of woodland the flowers seldom open wide.

CONFUSING SPECIES
Weak specimens of Broad-leaved Helleborine (*page 56*) in woodland and Dune Helleborine (*page 62*) in dune slacks.

HYBRIDS
None known.

HABITAT

Found on chalky soils in deep shade under Beech, often growing up through a dense carpet of Ivy or Dog's Mercury; on dry sandy soils under birch, Sweet Chestnut, Larch or pine; in wet coastal sand dunes, where it tends to occupy the low, dry hummocks, growing with Creeping Willow, Common Bird's-foot-trefoil and Red Fescue.

POLLINATION

Always self-fertilised, sometimes cleistogamous (fertilisation occurring in the unopened flower). Seed-set is effective and efficient.

CONSERVATION

Southern woodland sites seem to be in decline, while in the north and in western coastal areas populations appear to be increasing.

DISTRIBUTION
Absent from Scotland, but widely distributed especially in central southern England, west to Somerset and Hereford east to Norfolk and north to Yorkshire and Northumberland. Coastal sand dune sites occur in Wales in Glamorgan and Merioneth, and on the Lancashire coast. In Ireland it grows in Leitrim, Cavan and Fermanagh

Nationally Scarce
W(NI) Order Schedule 8

Ghost Orchid

Epipogium aphyllum

previously: *Epipogium gmelini*

Very rare

Height: up to 25 cm
No. of flowers: up to 6

FLOWERING PERIOD
June to October

FORMER RANGE

IDENTIFICATION

The extensive underground system of flattened and branched rhizomes bears a fanciful resemblance to coral, hence its old name of Spurred Coral-root. The flowering stem is 5–25 cm in height with a swollen base, and is pinkish marked with darker spots and lines. There are no leaves. Up to six large flowers are borne on short, untwisted stalks, so that the lip often points upwards. The ovary is large and globular. The yellowish petals and sepals are narrow, marked with tiny red spots, and tend to hang drooping downwards. The lip has a large triangular central lobe with a wavy margin. It is pink, with purple papillae on the inner surface, the outer surface and the fat spur at its base being marked with pinkish-purple streaks. The flowers have been described as both banana-scented and foetid. Flowering is said to follow a very wet spring.

CONFUSING SPECIES
None.

HYBRIDS
None known.

HABITAT

The plants lack chlorophyll, being entirely saprophytic, growing in deep leaf-litter in Beech woods where the ground is virtually bare of vegetation. They have been recorded rarely in oak woodland. The underground root system can be extensive, and one flowering spike has been recorded growing out of a decayed tree stump. Flowering is erratic and many years can pass without any flowers being produced, so nothing will be seen above ground.

POLLINATION

Bees have been reported as pollinators, but visits to plants in dark Beech woods must be infrequent. However, ripe seed capsules are produced.

CONSERVATION

In 1978 and 1979, several plants were dug up and removed. Slug damage is a problem unless the stems are protected. Plants are difficult to see against the background of dead Beech leaves and have been located by shining a bright torch beam parallel to the ground to highlight the flowering spikes.

DISTRIBUTION
Ghost Orchid was first recorded on the Herefordshire-Wiltshire border in 1854, but was dug up. It was recorded sporadically from Shropshire and Herefordshire until 1910 and again in 1982. In the Chilterns in Oxfordshire it flowered several times between 1924 and 1933, and was then discovered in Buckinghamshire in 1953. Occasional flowering has been recorded in both sites since, but there has been no reliable report in England since 1986.

CRITICALLY ENDANGERED
W&C Act Schedule 8

68

Bird's-nest Orchid

Neottia nidus-avis

Widespread

Height: up to 50 cm
No. of flowers: up to 100

IDENTIFICATION

The true rhizome is concealed in a mass of short, fleshy roots, resembling a badly made bird's nest, hence the common name. The stem is stout, up to 50 cm high, and is often accompanied by the dead stem and split seed capsules of the previous season's flower spike. The leaves are reduced to sheathing scales. All parts of the plant are a honey-brown colour, the flowering spike bearing as many as 100 closely-packed flowers. The petals and sepals are short, forming a hood above the broad, long lip. This is forked midway into two rounded, spreading lobes. There is a shallow cup full of nectar at the base of the lip, and the flowers have a pleasant scent of honey.

CONFUSING SPECIES
Superficially, could be mistaken for a broomrape (see *page 12*).

HYBRIDS
None known.

HABITAT
Like the Ghost Orchid (*page 68*), this species lacks chlorophyll and is entirely saprophytic, growing in deep humus particularly under Beech and Yew on chalk soils. It is sometimes accompanied by another saprophyte, the Yellow Bird's-nest. It also grows in mixed broad-leaved woodland and in Hazel coppices, but always where there is a deep layer of leaf-mould. It can tolerate heavy shade, but is never abundant, even in favoured sites.

POLLINATION
Small flies and thrips are attracted to the flowers and may disrupt the fragile, bright yellow pollen masses, leading to fertilisation. Self-fertilisation also occurs, sometimes in unopened flowers, and plants have been known to set seed without the flowering spike emerging above ground. Seed production is efficient, plants taking about nine years to reach maturity.

CONSERVATION
The most marked population decline has been in south-east England, due to disturbance by woodland clearance and the planting of conifers.

FLOWERING PERIOD
End of April to early July

DISTRIBUTION
Widespread throughout England, with the main centre of distribution in the south-east. It is widespread but uncommon in mainland Scotland, usually in Beech woods, and occurs on Mull. In Ireland it is widespread but scarce.

Common Twayblade

Listera ovata

may be re-named: *Neottia ovata*

Common

Height: up to 75 cm
No. of flowers: up to 100

FLOWERING PERIOD
Late April to July

IDENTIFICATION

The common name probably derives from Old Norse, since the modern Swedish name is Två Blad – two leaves. Most plants do have two dark green, oval leaves borne some way up the stem; rarely there may be three or even five leaves. The glandular hairy stem can be up to 75 cm tall. The lax flower spike may have as many as 100 small yellow-green flowers, with a globular ovary set on a long stalk. The upper petals and sepals form a loose hood above the long, forked lip, at the base of which is a nectar-secreting groove.

CONFUSING SPECIES
None, but abnormal flowers, such as those where all three petals resemble a lip, are not uncommon.

HYBRIDS
None known.

HABITAT
Occupies a wide range of habitats, from grassland and woodlands on both calcareous and mildly acid soils, to coastal dune slacks, limestone pavements and heathland. It also occurs in fens in England, Anglesey and Ireland, where it grows with both Early (*pages 112–117*) and Southern Marsh-orchids (*page 118*). It can be abundant where it does occur, and sometimes dominates the ground flora.

DISTRIBUTION
Widely distributed, often abundant, throughout Great Britain and Ireland, except for Shetland.

POLLINATION
The rostellum is very fragile and explodes on contact, glueing pollen onto the head of the visiting insect. Pollination has been recorded by male sawflies *Tenthredo atra*, male springtails *Apteris abdominator* and male ichneumons *Ichneumon insidiosus*. Bees are attracted by the nectar in the lip, but are too large to act as pollinators. The period from seed to maturity is long – up to 15 years – but vegetative reproduction by aerial shoots on the long rhizomes is frequent, so that plants of varying maturity stretch out in a line from the parent plant.

CONSERVATION
No particular conservation concerns.

Lesser Twayblade
Listera cordata
may be re-named: *Neottia cordata*

Locally abundant

Height: rarely over 10 cm
No. of flowers: up to 20

FLOWERING PERIOD
Mid-May to mid-August

IDENTIFICATION

A diminutive and charming version of Common Twayblade, the Lesser Twayblade rarely exceeds 10 cm in height, ranging from three to 25 cm. There are usually two small, heart-shaped leaves borne one third of the way up the reddish, hairy stem. They are apple-green in colour with a well-marked central rib, much resembling the first leaves of Bilberry. Robust plants with two basal and two stem leaves have been recorded in woodland. There are up to 20 flowers. The ovary is fat and globular, and the petals and sepals are blunt and spreading. The lip is long and slender, forked to midway, with two sharply-pointed lobes. Nectar is secreted in a central groove in the lip. All the floral parts can be an attractive, iridescent reddish-bronze colour. It is worth noting that the flowers maintain their shape and colour long after the carpel valves have opened and seed has been shed. In any colony there will be many non-flowering plants, which are easily overlooked.

CONFUSING SPECIES
None.

HYBRIDS
None known.

HABITAT

Most commonly found in rather wet and acidic conditions on moors and in bogs, often growing with *Sphagnum* mosses in the shelter of Heather or Bilberry bushes. It also grows on mossy ground under pine trees, especially in damp hollows in the ground. In Yorkshire, it has been found growing in rather dry moss under Juniper on limestone pavement.

POLLINATION

Female gnats *Sciara thomae*, small flies and ichneumons have all been recorded acting as pollinators, although self-fertilisation may also occur. Seed is set in a high percentage of flowers. Plants also multiply vegetatively.

CONSERVATION
No particular conservation concerns.

DISTRIBUTION
Most records are for Scotland, the Western Isles, Orkney and Shetland. It has recently been recorded more extensively in north Wales in Caernarvonshire and Merioneth. It has long been known in Devon and Somerset, and in scattered locations in both the north and the south of Ireland. Old records for Buckinghamshire (1980) and Sussex (1989) may represent plants introduced via planted Rhododendrons or Pine trees.

Autumn Lady's-tresses

Spiranthes spiralis
previously: *Spiranthes autumnalis*

Widespread but
decreasing

Height: up to 15 cm
No. of flowers: up to 20

FLOWERING PERIOD
Mid-August to end September

IDENTIFICATION

Has four or five bluish-green leaves in a flat rosette which forms in late autumn and withers before the flower spike emerges, so that there are no leaves at the base of the current flower spike. The stem is 5–15 cm tall, with several pale green bract-like scales, all parts of the flower spike being covered with tiny white hairs, giving it a frosted appearance. There are up to 20 trumpet-shaped white flowers arranged in a tight left- or right-handed spiral. The lip is gutter-shaped with a frilled edge, and has a green, nectar-secreting groove down the centre. The flowers are strongly scented of honey, especially in the evening.

CONFUSING SPECIES

This species flowers much later than the other two *Spiranthes* species. Summer Lady's-tresses (*page 78*) is regarded as extinct in Britain, while Irish Lady's-tresses (*page 80*) has flowers in three spiral ranks and occurs predominantly in Scotland.

HYBRIDS

None known.

HABITAT

Primarily a plant of dry, well-drained grassland on chalk or limestone soils, it can also flourish on cliff-tops near the sea, in calcareous sand dunes and on lawns, grass tennis courts and in churchyards where the mowing régime is sympathetic. Short grass is essential if it is to flourish, and under suitable circumstances it will reward with thousands of little white flowers.

POLLINATION

At least two bumblebee species are involved in pollination, and seed-set is good. However, it takes 11 years from seed for the first leaves to be formed and several more years for the plant to reach flowering maturity. Plants grown under laboratory conditions have produced flowers in five years. After flowering, it can persist for years underground, before emerging to flower again.

CONSERVATION

The unsympathetic mowing of lawns in late summer has contributed to the loss of this charming orchid from many of its former sites. It can remain for years in a non-flowering state, appearing in thousands if a site is left unmown. Overgrazing by sheep, and especially by Rabbits, can also be a problem.

DISTRIBUTION
Widely distributed in southern England and coastal Wales, including the Isle of Bardsey where it was discovered in 1984. It grows as far north as Lancashire, on the Isle of Man, and around the coast of Ireland and in The Burren. It is absent from Scotland. At one unusual site in north Norfolk it grows a few metres away from Creeping Lady's-tresses, which occurs in acid soil under planted Pine trees. It has decreased markedly in the past 80 years, as old grassland has been ploughed-up and grazing régimes have changed.

Summer Lady's-tresses

Spiranthes aestivalis

IDENTIFICATION

Summer Lady's-tresses has about six narrow, yellow-green base leaves and several narrow, sheathing stem leaves. The stem, which is 10–40 cm tall, carries 5–20 white flowers in a single spiral. The ovaries are hairless and smooth. The trumpet-shaped flowers are slender, elegant and slightly drooping – distinctly slimmer than those of the Irish Lady's-tresses (*pages 33* and *80*), while the lip is much broader than that of Autumn Lady's-tresses (*pages 33* and *76*).

CONFUSING SPECIES

Autumn Lady's-tresses avoids the wet, boggy habitat favoured by Summer Lady's-tresses, and Irish Lady's-tresses has only been recorded in Scotland, Ireland and north Devon.

HYBRIDS

None known.

HABITAT

First recorded in 1840 in the New Forest in Hampshire, where it grew in *Sphagnum* bogs with plants such as Black Bog-rush and Sweet Gale, which are clearly illustrated in the last known photograph taken in July 1937 (back endpaper). Some eight sites in two distinct areas were known, and all were on the edge of running water, and distinctly wet.

POLLINATION

The flowers are evening-scented, but pollination by moths has not been proven.

CONSERVATION

Draining of suitable areas was certainly a major contributory cause of its demise, but so was the collecting of specimens for herbaria. Some museum herbarium sheets have as many as six plants on them, complete with tubers, and this must have hastened the loss of this orchid from the British flora. In the Channel Islands, it disappeared from Guernsey in 1914 and Jersey in 1925, due to drainage and over-collection.

FLOWERING PERIOD
Mid-July to mid-August

DISTRIBUTION
Historically always restricted to the New Forest, Hampshire, with eight known sites. In 1900, local botanists counted a total of over 200 flowering spikes, but by 1930 only 20 could be found. The last proven flowering was in 1952, although in 1959 an eminent lepidopterist found a *Spiranthes* flowering in a wet tussocky field in late July some 800 m from an historic site. There were rumours of flowering in 1980, but these remain unproven

EXTINCT

Irish Lady's-tresses

Spiranthes romanzoffiana
previously: *Spiranthes gemmipara*

Local and scarce

Height: 10–30 cm
No. of flowers: up to 20

FLOWERING PERIOD
Early August to early September

IDENTIFICATION

Plants growing in Scotland and the north of Ireland have narrow, sheathing leaves, yellowish-green in colour, making non-flowering plants remarkably difficult to detect. The bracts are long, leafy and sheath the ovary. Plants growing in southern Ireland have broader, flatter leaves, and broader, flatter bracts which lie close together, almost overlapping each other. There are 15–20 creamy white flowers in three distinct spiral ranks. The Hawthorn-scented flowers are relatively large, the floral parts forming a fat, rounded tube, the upper segments flared up at the tips, while the lip folds down and is marked inside with green veins. All parts are covered in glandular hairs.

CONFUSING SPECIES
Autumn Lady's-tresses (*page 76*), which is absent from Scotland.

HYBRIDS
None known.

TAXONOMIC STATUS
It was once thought that plants from southern Ireland constituted a separate species *Sprianthes gemmipara*, but studies in North America have shown that this is not the case. However, recent work by the Royal Botanic Garden, Edinburgh has shown there to be two distinct genetic populations in Scotland.

HABITAT

Grows in damp meadows close to lakes and rivers, on the site of old lazy-beds, and is an active colonist of cut-away peat bogs in some Irish sites. It tends to avoid densely tussocky areas, and in several mainland Scottish sites it grows on the flat margins of lochs with *Sphagnum* mosses and Marsh Clubmoss which are inundated in winter. There is good anecdotal evidence that it flowers best following winter trampling by grazing animals.

POLLINATION

In Canada, bees act as pollinators, but this has not been proved in Britain. In one of the largest British populations no seed has been set for more than five years, and vegetative multiplication by buds on the root system is important.

CONSERVATION

Cessation of grazing by cattle can lead to its disappearance. The old farming pattern, where grazing was habitual from late September to May, appeared to suit the species.

DISTRIBUTION
Widely distributed across North America. First found in Ireland in west Cork and south Kerry in 1810, and in Scotland on Coll in 1921. In Ireland, it grows in Galway and Mayo, in Cork at the head of Bantry Bay and on the Garron Plateau in Co Antrim. In Scotland, it has now been found on Islay Colonsay, Mull, Tiree Ardnamurchan and Morvern, Barra and Vatersay, South Uist and Benbecula. It was found in its only English location in Devon in 1957. It is capable of reappearing at old sites after an apparent absence of many years.

Nationally Scarce
UK BAP Priority Species
W(NI) Order Schedule 8

Creeping Lady's-tresses

Goodyera repens

Locally abundant

Height: up to 35 cm
No. of flowers: up to 25

IDENTIFICATION

This species has a well-developed system of creeping rhizomes, from which arise rosettes of long-stalked, pointed-oval leaves with a well-marked network of pale veins. The flower spike, which is 8–35 cm tall, bears a single spiral row of up to 25 creamy white flowers, which are twisted so that most of them face in the same direction. The lateral sepals spread outwards, while the dorsal sepal and upper petals form a hood enclosing the bright orange anthers. The outer surface of all the sepals, bracts and upper stem are densely covered in glandular hairs. The lip is pointed, with a sac-like base which secretes nectar, and the flowers are sweetly-scented.

CONFUSING SPECIES

Different habitat preferences, the net-veined leaves and floral details are unlikely to lead to confusion with the *Spiranthes* species.

HYBRIDS

None known.

HABITAT

A plant of coniferous woodland, growing particularly well in the deep leaf-litter and moss under Scots Pine. It can also be found in old sand dunes, again under pine trees, and growing in more open habitat amongst Bell Heather – but always with pine trees nearby.

POLLINATION

Insect pollination is mostly by small bumblebees, including *Bombus pratorum*, and seed is set in a high proportion of capsules. However, there is also extensive vegetative multiplication.

CONSERVATION

Forest clearance can result in the destruction of populations. The plant flourishes best in years of good rainfall, and may fail to flower in very dry summers.

FLOWERING PERIOD
July and August

DISTRIBUTION
Although distributed throughout the northern hemisphere, in Britain it is mainly known from north-east Scotland especially in remnants of the old Caledonian Forest of Strathspey and Caithness. It grows as far south as Westmorland and has an outlying population centre in north Norfolk, where it grows in several sites under planted pine trees. It is uncertain whether it was introduced there with Pine seedlings or has arisen naturally from airborne seed. It is absent from Ireland, Orkney, Shetland and the Western Isles

Fen Orchid

Liparis loeselii

Very rare

Height: up to 20 cm
No. of flowers: up to 18

IDENTIFICATION

FLOWERING PERIOD
Mid-June to early July

There are two forms, both of which have two bright, shiny, yellow-green leaves which overlap at their bases and sheath the hard pseudobulb formed at the base of the stem.

The **Fen form** has leaves which are 4× as long as they are broad. The flowering stem, 5–20 cm tall, is three-sided in the upper half. Four to 18 shining yellow-green flowers are carried rather close to the stem, some being rotated so that the lip points upwards. The sepals and upper petals are all long and narrow, while the lip is like a broad spearhead in shape, folded into a gutter. There is no nectar and no scent.

Var. *ovata*, the dune slack form, has broad leaves only 1·5× as long as they are wide, and a dumpy inflorescence whose flowers have much shorter sepals and petals. Most spikes only carry three to six flowers.

<small>CONFUSING SPECIES:</small> None.   <small>HYBRIDS:</small> None known.

HABITAT

The two forms exist in two distinct habitats. The fen form grows in basic or alkaline fens or on the edge of old peat cuttings, occupying the edges of pools where the vegetation of rushes, sedges and mosses is at an early stage of colonisation. Var. *ovata* grows in wet coastal dune slacks. To persist it requires a constant succession of new, immature slacks to be created, so that it can colonise new areas nearby as the old slacks mature and dry out.

POLLINATION

Pollination is assisted by rain. The anther cap on the top of the erect column is like a little hinged lid and raindrops striking the anther cap bang it down on the pollinia and push pollen onto the stigma. Seed is set in a high percentage of capsules, the ripe capsules being held erect as the flowers wither.

CONSERVATION

Scrub growth and widespread lowering of the water-table by drainage work over the last 100 years have wiped out many of the East Anglian populations. Active management is required to maintain vegetation at an early stage of colonisation. Var. *ovata* has suffered where the dunes have stabilised too well, and the necessary succession of newly formed dune slacks has failed. The dune variety is also sensitive to dry conditions and liable to damage by slugs. See the *Conservation in action* section on *page 168.*

DISTRIBUTION

Formerly known from a number of sites in Norfolk, Suffolk and Cambridgeshire, but now restricted to three sites in east Norfolk which are being actively managed to conserve the species. Var. *ovata* occurs on the coastal sand dunes of south Wales in Glamorgan and Carmarthen, and at two sites on the north Devon coast. It can grow in good numbers when conditions are favourable. Var. *ovata* had long been considered a British speciality, but has recently been discovered in north-west France

ENDANGERED
EC Habs Dir. Annexes II & IV
W&C Act Schedule 8
UK BAP Priority Species

fen

ova

Bog Orchid

Hammarbya paludosa
previously: *Malaxis paludosa;*
may be re-named: *Liparis paludosa*

IDENTIFICATION

A tiny, 3–12 cm high, orchid with a five-angled stem. There are two pseudobulbs at the base of the stem; the lower one with remnants of the leaves left from the previous season, the upper with two small, oval, green leaves, whose bases overlap and sheath it. The upper leaves frequently have a fringe of minute bulbils, which easily break off and float away in the surface water, resulting in vegetative propagation. The flowers are unusual in that the lip always points upwards, having rotated a full 360° from the primitive position, whereas in most other orchids the lip lies ventrally, the flower having rotated through 180°. There are up to 15 flowers, barely 3 mm long. The pointed lip is marked with alternate longitudinal stripes of light and dark green, and there is a small nectar-secreting area at the base. The lateral petals fold right back, wrapping round the base of the flower, which may smell faintly of cucumber.

CONFUSING SPECIES   HYBRIDS
None.   None known.

HABITAT

Most often to be found in established *Sphagnum* bogs where the water is acidic. In many cases, Bog Orchid grows in floating carpets of bog-mosses, a habitat which is easily damaged by human intrusion and one which can reward the unwary botanist with sudden immersion! It can also be found growing in moss on the edges of runnels and flushes in mountains up to 500 m, such flushes often appearing a vivid green. Occasionally, Bog Orchid is found in running water on the edge of stony tracks, where moss growth is scant.

POLLINATION

Pollination is by the gnat *Sciara thomae* and possibly by small flies and midges which are such a feature of bogs in summer. Pollinia are removed in most flowers, and seed-set is efficient. The seed is dust-like, and disperses on the water surface.

CONSERVATION

Drainage work has caused a dramatic decline in populations in all areas, but especially in southern England. As the plant is so tiny and insignificant, it is likely that it has been overlooked and has therefore been under-recorded.

86

Rare

Height: up to 12 cm
No. of flowers: up to 15

FLOWERING PERIOD
July to mid-September
(plants at high altitude
flower later)

DISTRIBUTION
Many counties in southern England have lost their Bog Orchids. It can still be found in the New Forest in Hampshire, in Dorset, Devon and Cornwall, in Wales, Cumbria and in Scotland, especially in the north and west. It also occurs in the Western Isles, Shetland and sparsely in the north-west and east of Ireland.

W(NI) Order Schedule 8

Coralroot Orchid
Corallorhiza trifida

Local

Height: up to 28 cm
No. of flowers: up to 13

IDENTIFICATION
Coralroot Orchid is saprophytic, and is named after its creamy, knobbly, coral-like mass of rhizomes. There are no true roots, but tufts of hairs. The plants are heavily dependant upon mycorrhizal fungus, although there is a little chlorophyll in the stem and ovaries which allows some photosynthesis. The plant grows entirely underground until it flowers, the stem, which is 6–28 cm tall, has no leaves except for two to four greenish-yellow sheaths. Most parts are yellow-green, although plants growing in dune slacks may have a reddish tinge. There are 4–13 drooping flowers with strap-shaped, incurving sepals, the tips of which are reddish-brown and look as if they have been scorched. The upper sepal and two upper petals form a hood. The lip has two small side lobes and a broad white central lobe with a frilly edge, the base marked with bright crimson spots. Peloric plants, where the three petals are all lip-shaped, have been recorded in Fife and Morayshire, with an old record from the west of Edinburgh in 1824.

FLOWERING PERIOD
May to August

CONFUSING SPECIES	HYBRIDS
None.	None known.

HABITAT
Most often to be found in damp, shaded Alder and willow carr, and on the margins of lowland lochs. It also grows in damp dune slacks with Creeping Willow and less frequently in birch and pine forest on sand, where it flowers in the deep litter of pine needles and moss with Creeping Lady's-tresses (*page 82*) and Lesser Twayblade (*page 74*). In Morayshire, it has colonised the edges of 'winter lochs' left by shingle extraction, which dry out in summer to create dune slack type communities.

POLLINATION
There is virtually no nectar, and scent is faint. Insects such as hoverflies and dung flies of the genus *Scathophaga* visit the flowers, but do not appear to remove pollen. The pollen is extremely crumbly and it is likely that insects simply dislodge it, to fall on the stigma. Seed-set is highly efficient at 85–100%.

CONSERVATION
Coralroot Orchid is not easy to spot in vegetation. Given its erratic flowering pattern and lack of 'above-ground' structures, other than when flowering, it is probably under-recorded.

DISTRIBUTION
The main population centre is eastern and north-east Scotland. It is absent from the Western Isles, Orkney and Shetland, and also from Wales and Ireland. Further south it occurs in Cumbria and in two sites in Yorkshire, where it flowers intermittently. Old records in England include one from the suburbs north of Newcastle.

Musk Orchid

Herminium monorchis

Decreasing, may be locally abundant

Height: up to 15 cm
No. of flowers: up to 20

IDENTIFICATION

Musk Orchid is a diminutive plant 5–15 cm (rarely 30cm) tall, and is hard to spot until you recognise the bright yellow-green colour. It has two or three strap-shaped basal leaves and one pointed stem leaf. Most spikes carry no more than 20 densely-packed flowers, all the sepals and petals being pointed and toothed, so that the floret appears as a spiky bell-shape. The lip is three-lobed, with a long central lobe; at the base is a shallow nectar-secreting cup, in reality a primitive spur. The flowers have a strong honey scent, but certainly do not smell of musk! It has one main, spherical tuber and a number of smaller satellite tubers connected by very slender stolons. These connections are fragile and can easliy be broken. If this happens, it can appear to have one round tuber, as the scientific name implies. The satellite tubers help to spread and produce clumps of flower spikes.

CONFUSING SPECIES
The only similar orchid, the Bog Orchid (*page 86*), grows in a completely different habitat.

HYBRIDS
None known.

HABITAT
The habitat requirements are very precise: it grows in very short turf on chalk downs or over oolitic limestone, favouring the contour-hugging terracettes produced by sheep on steep, sunny slopes, and also abandoned chalk quarries.

POLLINATION
The flowers are highly attractive to insects, but the pollinators have to be tiny (up to 1 mm long) in order to enter the minute flowers. Tiny parasitic wasps *Tetrastichus diaphantus*, flies and the soldier beetle *Malthodes pumilus* have been shown to act as pollinators. Although self-fertilisation has not been proven to occur at all regularly, the level of seed-set is high.

CONSERVATION
The ploughing-up of old grassland, and scrub encroachment resulting from a reduction in sheep grazing, has resulted in the loss of this species from much of East Anglia and many sites in southern England. Being very shallow-rooted, it seems to be highly sensitive to drought conditions; the hot summer of 1976, for example, having led to the decline in many populations.

FLOWERING PERIOD
Mid-June to early August

DISTRIBUTION
Musk Orchid is restricted entirely to southern and south-eastern England, particularly the South Downs of Sussex, the North Downs of Kent and Surrey, the Chilterns and the Cotswolds. It also occurs on the chalk downs of Hampshire and Wiltshire.

Nationally Scarce

Greater Butterfly-orchid

Platanthera chlorantha

previously: *Habenaria chlorantha* and *Habenaria virescens*

Widespread but decreasing

Height: up to 60 cm
No. of flowers: up to 40

FLOWERING PERIOD
May to July

IDENTIFICATION

Plants growing in the open are robust, while those in shaded woodland are taller and more slender. The flower spike, 20–60 cm tall, has two large, elliptical, shiny, bluish-green basal leaves and up to five smaller, pointed stem leaves. There are 10–40 white flowers in an open spike, the flowers borne well away from the stem on S-shaped ovaries. The ovate, wavy-edged lateral sepals spread outwards and downwards, the smaller upper sepal and two petals forming a broad, semicircular hood. The translucent lip is long and strap-shaped with a greenish tip, the spur at the base being up to 25 mm long, lying right across the flower spike and curving slightly downwards. The two pollinia diverge and are set wide apart at the base of the column, giving a clear view down into the spur. The scent is sweet and strong, particularly at night. The white flowers are highly reflective and show up well in dim light.

DISTRIBUTION
Widely distributed in southern England, Wales, north-west England, western Scotland and the northern half of Ireland. It is absent from Orkney, Shetland and the Outer Hebrides.

CONFUSING SPECIES

Lesser Butterfly-orchid (*page 94*) is very similar, but the two pollinia are parallel and lie close together, obscuring the entrance to the spur. Aberrant flowers are not uncommon: some lack both lip and spur, others have no lateral sepals but a sepaloid lip with no spur, yet others have a spur but no lip. Flowers with all three petals resembling a lip, complete with spur, have been recorded in Skye.

HYBRIDS

Hybrids between the two butterfly-orchids have been confirmed in Scotland. The so-called hybrid with Small-white Orchid in Scotland proved to be a peloric Greater Butterfly-orchid.

HABITAT
Most commonly found on well-drained, calcareous soils, on downland, old pastures, hill hay meadows, woodland such as that on the heavier soils below chalk hills, and occasionally in calcareous sand dunes. Rarely found on slightly acid moorland.

POLLINATION

Although bumblebees visit the flowers, they have too short a proboscis to reach the nectar in the spur. Pollinators include Silver-Y moth and Elephant and Small Elephant Hawk-moths. Seed is set in 70–90% of capsules.

CONSERVATION

Many sites were lost to woodland clearance and the improvement of upland pastures during the last century. The development of a dense woodland canopy suppresses flowering, but subsequent clearance can lead to a dramatic reappearance of hundreds of flower spikes, even after an interval of more than 50 years.

Lesser Butterfly-orchid

Platanthera bifolia
previously: *Habenaria bifolia*

Widespread but decreasing

Height: up to 55 cm
No. of flowers: up to 25

FLOWERING PERIOD
Mid-May to July

IDENTIFICATION

Plants growing in woodland are slender, while those on hill sites in the open are rather dumpy. Although similar to Greater Butterfly-orchid (*page 92*), with a flower spike of 15–55 cm and up to five small pointed stem leaves, the two shining green basal leaves, especially of the hill form, are shorter and broader. There are some 25 white flowers tinged with yellow-green in a slim flower spike. The upper sepal and petals form a loose, triangular hood above the pollinia, which lie parallel and close together, obscuring the opening into the spur, which is long and almost straight. The flowers are night-scented, but the chemical components of the scent are different to those of Greater Butterfly-orchid and attract different pollinators.

CONFUSING SPECIES

There is no difference in size between the two butterfly-orchids, but the flower spike of Lesser Butterfly-orchid appears slimmer, as the ovary is shorter and the flowers are held closer to the stem. Lesser Butterfly-orchid can be distinguished reliably from Greater Butterfly-orchid by examining the pollinia – in Lesser they lie parallel and close together.

HYBRIDS

Hybrids between the two butterfly-orchids are rare, as are those between Lesser Butterfly-orchid and other species. However, hybrids have been recorded with Frog Orchid in South Uist (1949) and with Common and Heath Spotted-orchids.

POLLINATION

Sphingid moths are attracted by the scent, and tend to hover in front of the flowers, resting their forelegs on the lip. As the proboscis enters the spur it pushes between the pollinia, dislodging the sticky discs which adhere to it. Pollinators include Pine, Small Elephant and, to a lesser extent, Elephant Hawk-moths.

CONSERVATION

This species has suffered a serious decline, especially in central and southern England, as a result of woodland clearance. Upland populations in the north and west have suffered from overgrazing.

DISTRIBUTION
Widespread on the west side of Britain from Cornwall to north Scotland, but absent or uncommon elsewhere. Found in Orkney for the first time in 1985. Similarly in Ireland it is more common in the north and north-west, but rare in the south and east.

HABITAT
Occupies a wide range of habitats, being far more tolerant of acid conditions than Greater Butterfly-orchid. Found in grassland, woodland (especially Beech woods in southern England), in hill pastures up to 400 m, on heaths and moorland, and in tussocky marshy ground.

Pyramidal Orchid
Anacamptis pyramidalis
previously: *Orchis pyramidalis*

Locally common

Height: up to 60 cm
No. of flowers: up to 100

FLOWERING PERIOD
Mid-June to August

IDENTIFICATION
At first, the flower spike is pyramidal in shape, hence the common name, although it can elongate into more of a cylinder as the flower spike matures. There are three to four narrow, grey-green basal leaves, often shrivelled by mid summer, and up to six narrow stem leaves. The stem, 10–60 cm tall, bears a spike of 50–100 tightly-packed pink flowers; plants by the sea have much darker coloured flowers. White-flowered plants **alb** are rare, and make a striking contrast with their neighbours. The blunt lateral sepals are spreading, whereas the dorsal sepal and upper petals forming a tight hood. The lip is deeply three-lobed, the lobes varying greatly in shape, and bears two erect converging plates at the base, which direct the proboscis of a visiting insect into the long, straight spur. The flowers have a faint sweet scent. Plants with unlobed lips, var. *emarginata* **em**, were first described in Sussex in 1974, and have since been found in Hampshire and in calcareous sand dunes in Ireland.

CONFUSING SPECIES
None; it is a very distinctive species.

HYBRIDS
The hybrid with Fragrant Orchid has been rarely, and rather dubiously, recorded.

HABITAT
Grows in well-drained calcareous soils, and can be abundant on chalk downs, dune slacks, seaside golf links, cliff tops and on limestone pavement. It is a robust colonist and can add a welcome splash of colour to roadside verges, abandoned quarries and even industrial wasteland. It is also persistent, and has been recorded from one downland site in Kent since 1871.

POLLINATION
Large Skipper butterflies, Six-spot Burnet moths, Buff-tailed Bumblebees and Forester moths have all been recorded as pollinators. The two pollinia are joined into a saddle-shaped viscid disc, which is easily disturbed by the visiting insect and instantly clamps round the proboscis. Seed is set in up to 95% of capsules.

CONSERVATION
Although sites have been lost to agriculture, this has been offset to some extent by its colonisation of roadside verges.

DISTRIBUTION
Pyramidal Orchid is widespread on chalk and limestone in southern and eastern England, north to Northumberland. In north and south Wales it appears to be spreading in the coastal dunes. In Scotland it is far less common, recorded from a few mainland sites in the Borders, Fife, Kintyre and the south-west coast. It has recently been recorded in machair grassland on South Uist, Barra, Coll, Tiree, Mull and Canna. In Ireland it is more common on limestone soils in the central counties.

alb

em

Small-white Orchid

Pseudorchis albida

previously: *Leucorchis albida, Gymnadenia albida* and
Habenaria albida

IDENTIFICATION

Small-white Orchid tends to grow singly or in small groups,
and is easily overlooked. There are three or four fairly broad,
flat basal leaves, and one or two narrow, pointed stem leaves.
The flower spike, 10–40 cm high, usually bears 30–40 small,
ivory white, bell-shaped flowers in a tightly-packed cylinder.
Occasionally, plants with more than 100 flowers can be found.
The small, blunt sepals and petals form a loose hood, from
which protrudes the three-lobed lip, the central lobe being
longer. There is a thick conical, down-curved spur 2–3 mm
long, and the flowers are vanilla-scented.

CONFUSING SPECIES

Several suspected sightings in southern England have turned
out to be white Pyramidal Orchids (*page 96*).

HYBRIDS

The hybrid with Fragrant Orchid has been recorded at
Rothiemurchus (2000) and several other sites in Scotland, as
well as in Yorkshire. The hybrid with Heath Spotted-orchid has
been found in Orkney.

HABITAT

Grows in sunny, well-drained mountain pastures up to 700 m,
on cliff ledges and, less frequently, on moorland after a 'burn',
before the regrowth of Heather overwhelms it. It tolerates a
wide range of soil conditions, from Carboniferous limestone to
moderately acid soil. In Sussex, where it was last seen in the
1930s, the habitat was composed of a mosaic of small grazed
pastures and woodland, now long gone under housing
development. It is often accompanied by Fragrant Orchid,
Lesser Butterfly-orchid and Heath Spotted-orchid.

POLLINATION

The flowers are visited by butterflies, day-flying moths and
solitary bees, but no positive identification of the species
involved has been made. It is probable that self-fertilisation also
occurs, and seed-set is efficient (*ca.* 90%).

CONSERVATION

Overgrazing and habitat destruction have led to the loss of
many populations, particularly in southern England. Losses
continue, but new sites are being found due to better recording.

Locally common

Height: up to 40 cm
No. of flowers: up to 100

FLOWERING PERIOD
End of May to mid-July

DISTRIBUTION
Small-white Orchid is
never abundant, occurring
in a few sites in central
and north Wales, in west
Yorkshire and
Northumberland.
In Scotland, it occurs with
increasing frequency
further north, particularly
in the north-west.
It is absent from Shetland
and the Outer Hebrides.
In Ireland it is found mainly
in northern counties and
in Galway.
In Tipperary it reappeared
in 1991, having last been
recorded there in 1898,
and a similar reappearance
was recorded in west
Yorkshire after an interval
of more than 50 years.

W(NI) Order Schedule 8

Fragrant Orchid

Gymnadenia conopsea sub-species *conopsea*
previously: *Habenaria conopsea*

Height: up to 40 cm
No. of flowers: up to 200

FLOWERING PERIOD
Mid-May to early August

Fragrant Orchid is widely distributed throughout the British Isles, but exists in three distinct forms which at present are given sub-specific rank. In view of ongoing research work, these may well be split into three separate species. The most reliable features used to identify them are the shape of the lip and the size and position of the lateral sepals. Colour can vary greatly in all three sub-species, from pale to very dark pink; albino flowers **alb** are not uncommon. The sub-species *densiflora* and *borealis* are shown overleaf.

Orange shows the known range of the Fragrant Orchid complex; purple shows the known range of the sub-species *conopsea*.

IDENTIFICATION

A moderate-sized plant, 10–40 cm tall, with three to five long, narrow, folded basal leaves and several narrow, pointed stem leaves. There are as many as 200 densely-packed pink flowers in a long, slim spike, each with a very long, down-curved spur full of nectar. The lateral sepals are narrow, pointed and droop down at an angle of 30°. The lip is clearly divided into three rounded lobes, the central lobe being the longest. The plant has a sickly-sweet scent.

Confusing Species

The other pink-flowering downland species, Pyramidal Orchid (*page 96*), can be distinguished by the shape of the flower spike and by the two guide plates at the base of the lip.

Hybrids

The following species have all been recorded as hybrids with Fragrant Orchid: Lesser Butterfly-orchid, Pyramidal, Small-white and Frog Orchids, Common and Heath Spotted-orchids (see photographs on *page 161*), and Northern Marsh-orchid.

POLLINATION

Butterflies and day-flying moths are strongly attracted to the flowers. Six-spot Burnet moths, Large Skipper butterflies and several species of bumblebee have all been recorded as pollinators, some falling prey to the numerous crab-spiders which lurk in the flower spikes. Most flowers have one or both pollinia removed and seed-set is efficient.

CONSERVATION

Habitat destruction by ploughing, drainage or overgrazing can decimate populations. In many downland areas in southern England, coarse grasses such as Tor-grass have spread, suppressing flowering, but recent schemes using grazing with Exmoor ponies have resulted in a gratifying blaze of pink flowers.

HABITAT AND DISTRIBUTION
This form is quite restricted in its range, growing on the chalk grasslands of Kent, Sussex and Surrey west to the Cotswolds, Mendips and Devon, where it was found on the north coast in 1988 - the first record there since 1912. It occurs northwards on Oolitic limestone in Northamptonshire, Lincolnshire and Yorkshire, and on Magnesian limestone near Ripon. There are only two authoritative records from Scotland: in Banffshire and in Caithness. In Ireland it is frequent in the central counties.

alb

Fragrant Orchid – sub-species *densiflora* and *borealis*
Gymnadenia conopsea

At present the three distinct forms of Fragrant Orchid are regarded as sub-species but, in the light of ongoing research, may be split into three separate species. The most reliable features used to identify them are the shape of the lip and the size and position of the lateral sepals. The nominate sub-species *conopsea* is described and illustrated on page 98; the other two sub-species are described and illustrated here.

(den) Sub-species *densiflora*

IDENTIFICATION
Robust, up to 75 cm tall, with many basal leaves and a densely-packed spike of large flowers. The colour of the flowers varies from pale mauve to dark pink. The lateral sepals are straight with blunt tips and inrolled edges, and are held horizontally. The lip is broad and flat with distinct 'shoulders', the central lobe being poorly defined and not exceeding the lateral lobes. The scent is sweet – rather like that of carnations. Where this form grows with ssp. *conopsea* it tends to flower two weeks later.

HABITAT & DISTRIBUTION
This sub-species is found in base-rich fens and damp meadows, but also occurs on north-facing chalk downland slopes with moist seepage areas. It occurs widely in southern England from Sussex to Somerset, northwards to Hereford-shire and Staffordshire, in Cambridgeshire, Suffolk and Norfolk in the east, and in Cardiganshire and Anglesey in Wales. The most northerly site in England is on the border of Yorkshire and Westmorland. In Scotland it is known only from one site on the west coast of Wester Ross, and in Peebles, where it was found in 2000. In Ireland it grows mainly in the west.

Local

Height:	up to 75 cm
No. of flowers:	up to 200

FLOWERING PERIOD
Mid-May to early August

Orange shows the known range of the Fragrant Orchid complex; purple shows the known range of the sub-species *densiflora*.

(bor) Sub-species *borealis*

IDENTIFICATION
A short plant, 10–15 cm in height, with a fairly open spike of 20–30 small flowers, varying in colour from pale mauve to dark pink – often darker in sites by the sea. The lateral sepals are small, flat and pointed, held at a slight angle downwards. The lip is disproportionately small, with two small side lobes and a longer central lobe. The spur is smaller than that of the other forms. The scent is strong and sweet, reminiscent of cloves.

HABITAT & DISTRIBUTION
This sub-species grows in a wide range of habitats, from base-rich to mildly acidic grasslands, heaths and moors up to 700 m. It is the commonest form in Scotland, where it is widely distributed. In south-west England it can be found on Exmoor, Dartmoor and the Lizard Peninsula in Cornwall. It has also been recorded from Cardiganshire in Wales, and in Ireland from both the west and north-east in Antrim and Londonderry. Elsewhere in England, there are small populations in the New Forest in Hampshire, Ashdown Forest in Sussex and on downland in Sussex and Wiltshire.

Locally common

Height:	up to 15 cm
No. of flowers:	up to 30

FLOWERING PERIOD
Mid-May to early August

Orange shows the known range of the Fragrant Orchid complex; purple shows the known range of the sub-species *borealis*.

Data Deficient

Frog Orchid

Coeloglossum viride
previously: *Habenaria viridis*;
may be re-named: *Dactylorhiza viridis*

Local

Height: up to 15 cm
No. of flowers: up to 50

FLOWERING PERIOD
Late June to early September,
rarely from mid-May in
coastal southern England

IDENTIFICATION
Most plants are 5–15 cm tall, rarely up to 30 cm. There are three to five strap-shaped basal leaves and several pointed stem leaves. The flower spike is compact, with up to 50 flowers, some plants having very long, prominent bracts. The flowers vary in colour from yellow-green **grn** to red-brown **red** in drier sites, the sepals and petals forming a tight globose hood. The lip is long, strap-shaped and three-lobed, the central lobe being small and shorter than the laterals; they are said to resemble frogs. The lip is usually paler in colour, folded back under the ovary, and bears a small, blunt spur. There is a faint honey scent.

CONFUSING SPECIES
None.

HYBRIDS
Hybrids are rare but have been recorded with Common Spotted-orchid (see photograph on *page 161*) in Wiltshire, the Isle of Lewis in the Hebrides and Co. Down in Ireland; with Southern Marsh-orchid in Hampshire; Northern Marsh-orchid in Scotland; and with Fragrant Orchid and Lesser Butterfly-orchid in several counties.

HABITAT
Frog Orchid grows in dry, well-grazed, base-rich grassland, where the grass is short. It is found on chalk downs, especially on old earthworks and barrow-mounds, in chalk quarries, calcareous sand dunes, on golf courses, and is a feature of the machair grasslands of the Hebrides. It also grows on limestone pavement and rocky ledges up to 1,000 m in Scotland. The number of flowering plants can fluctuate widely from year to year, but individuals can flower for at least seven years consecutively.

POLLINATION
Continental authorities describe various butterflies, ichneumonid wasps and beetles acting as pollinators, but data are scarce for this species in Britain. However, the click beetle *Athous haemorrhoidalis* has been seen removing pollinia.

CONSERVATION
A reduction in grazing of favoured grasslands can lead to its temporary disappearance.

DISTRIBUTION
Frog Orchid is widely distributed in north and west Britain and north and west Ireland, although the number of sites is relatively small. It has declined markedly in central England and East Anglia and has disappeared in recent years from its only site in Kent. It is present in reasonable numbers on the chalk hills from Sussex to Wiltshire, with a few scattered sites west to south Devon and Cornwall.

red

Common Spotted-orchid

Dactylorhiza fuchsii

previously: *Orchis fuchsii* and *Orchis maculata*

Common Spotted-orchid possesses one very attractive variety and two sub-species, each with a limited distribution. The normal form is described below; the other forms are described and illustrated on the following page.

IDENTIFICATION

Can grow up to 70 cm tall in sheltered locations. There are numerous narrow, pointed basal leaves and three to five clasping stem leaves. The leaves are usually spotted or blotched with purplish-brown marks; there is considerable variation in these markings. The bracts are pointed and longer than the ovary. The flower spike of numerous pale lilac or pink flowers is closely-packed and tapers at the tip. The lateral sepals are spreading, the dorsal sepal and upper petals forming a loose hood. All are marked with lines and dots. The lip has three well-defined lobes, the lateral lobes being rhomboidal in shape, and the central lobe longer and triangular. The lip is marked with a symmetrical double loop enclosing a series of lines and dots, while the spur is straight and slender – in contrast to the fat, conical spur of the marsh-orchids. White flowers with yellow pollinia (alb) are not uncommon, but can be confused with very faintly marked flowers where the bursicles around the pollinia are pale mauve.

CONFUSING SPECIES

Heath Spotted-orchid (*page 110*) has narrower leaves with smaller spots and a more triangular flower spike. Its flowers have a broader lip with a small central lobe and smaller markings which extend across the whole lip surface and do not form a distinct double loop.

HYBRIDS

Hybridises with all three forms of Fragrant Orchid, also with Frog Orchid, rarely with Early Marsh-orchid and more frequently with Southern, Northern, Western and Narrow-leaved Marsh-orchids. The hybrid with Heath Spotted-orchid has been reported but is difficult to identify with certainty. Photographs of most of these hybrids are shown on *page 161*.

POLLINATION

Pollinators include hoverflies, female Cuckoo Bees, Buff-tailed Bumblebees and the beetle *Dascillus cervinus*. Seed-set is efficient, and plants also multiply vegetatively to form clumps.

CONSERVATION

The plant can rapidly colonise suitable habitat.

Locally abundant

Height:	up to 70 cm
No. of flowers:	up to 150

FLOWERING PERIOD
Mid-May to early August

DISTRIBUTION

The normal form is widespread throughout Britain and Ireland, except in Devon and Cornwall and in north-east Scotland. It is absent from Orkney. The other sub-species and the colour form have restricted distributions (see *page 108*).

HABITAT

Widespread in calcareous and neutral grasslands, in open woodlands, in old quarries, on railway banks and road verges throughout Britain and Ireland. It avoids truly acid soils, but has proved capable of colonising waste ground and abandoned industrial sites.

alb

Common Spotted-orchid – varieties and sub-species

Dactylorhiza fuchsii
previously: *Orchis fuchsii* and *Orchis maculata*

Common Spotted-orchid possesses one very attractive variety and two sub-species, each with a limited distribution. These are described below and illustrated opposite. The normal form is covered on the previous two pages.

(rho) Var. *rhodochila*

IDENTIFICATION
The whole lip is a uniform dark reddish-purple, so no markings are evident. The leaves are heavily spotted, even entirely brownish-bronze in colour.

DISTRIBUTION
First recorded in north Lincolnshire in 1979, and since from Sussex, Surrey, Nottinghamshire, Durham and Fife. There is also a herbarium specimen in Sussex dating from 1870.

(heb) Sub-species: *hebridensis*

IDENTIFICATION
A dwarf plant up to 15 cm in height, with finely-marked leaves. The flower spike is short, densely packed with large rosy-pink flowers. The lip is three-lobed with a longer triangular central lobe, with the spots and lines extending across the whole surface, but not forming distinct loops.

DISTRIBUTION
Characteristic of the machair grassland of the Western Isles, where it forms great drifts of colour in late June. Recorded from the Outer Hebrides, Jura, Tiree, Sutherland, Shetland, Donegal, Galway, Kerry and east Cornwall.

(oke) Sub-species: *okellyi*

IDENTIFICATION
The leaves are slender and unspotted. The flower stem, up to 30 cm tall, bears strongly-scented white flowers in a square-topped spike. They are white or very faintly marked, while the lobes of the lip are rounded and almost equal.

DISTRIBUTION
A plant of calcareous grassland, where it grows in small colonies (single, white-flowered Common Spotted-orchids are unlikely to be this sub-species). Recorded from Counties Down, Fermanagh, Leitrim, Clare and Galway in Ireland, also from the Isle of Man and the Scottish islands of Coll, Tiree and Kintyre.

Heath Spotted-orchid

Dactylorhiza maculata sub-species *ericetorum*
previously: *Orchis ericetorum, Orchis elodes* and
Orchis maculata

Widely distributed,
locally abundant

Height: up to 40 cm
No. of flowers: up to 50

FLOWERING PERIOD
Late May to early August

IDENTIFICATION

Can be robust, with a slightly ridged stem up to 40 cm tall, but most plants are smaller and elegant, 10–15 cm tall, with a rather pyramidal-shaped flower spike. It tends to grow in clumps. There are four to eight narrow, pointed base leaves, lightly marked with small spots or circles. It usually has 5–20 pale pinkish-mauve, faintly scented flowers, although plants in favoured southern localities may have more than 50. The lateral sepals are spreading, the dorsal sepal and upper petals forming a loose hood. The lip is broad and skirt-like, with a small triangular central lobe, marked with a series of red lines and small dots which never form the well-defined double loops typical of the Common Spotted-orchid (*page 106*). The spur is slim and straight. White flowers **alb** are not uncommon, nor are deep, heavily-marked ones, and most large populations contain these forms. Flowers with plain, dark red lips, like var. *rhodochila* of Common Spotted-orchid (*page 108*), have been recorded in Merioneth.

DISTRIBUTION

Flourishes particularly in the west and north-west of Britain, and similarly in the west and north of Ireland. It is less common in the Midlands and south-east England, where it is becoming scarce.

CONFUSING SPECIES

The shape of the lip and its markings should distinguish it from Common Spotted-orchid. Dwarf plants in the Outer Hebrides can be confused with the equally dwarf *hebridensis* sub-species **heb** of Common Spotted-orchid (*page 108*). In the south of England, Heath Spotted-orchid flowers two weeks later than Common, but in the north and north-west this situation tends to be reversed.

HYBRIDS

Hybrids with Common Spotted-orchid are not infrequent, and are often obvious due to their larger size and vigorous growth. Hybrids have also been recorded with Small-white and Fragrant Orchids; Early, Southern, Northern, Western and Narrow-leaved Marsh-orchids; and dubiously with Lesser Butterfly-orchid. Photographs of many of these hybrids are shown on *pages 161–162*.

HABITAT

Typically a plant of acid soils, growing in well-drained habitats such as grassland, moors and heaths, from sea-level to 900 m. Also found in the wetter surroundings of bogs, usually on slightly raised areas which are not saturated. Very rarely found on limestone

POLLINATION

Bumblebees and butterflies have occasionally been recorded as pollinators, but most active are Bristle Flies and the long-legged true fly *Ptychoptera contaminata*. The level of seed-set is high.

CONSERVATION

Although one of the commonest orchids in the north and north-west, habitat destruction has led to its decline in places.

Early Marsh-orchid

Dactylorhiza incarnata

previously: *Orchis latifolia, Orchis incarnata* and *Orchis strictifolia*

Early Marsh-orchid is widely distributed throughout the British Isles. It is represented by five sub-species which are very different in colour and have distinct habitat preferences – and hence a different pattern of distribution. The 'nominate' sub-species *incarnata* is described on this page; the other forms are described and illustrated on the following four pages.

IDENTIFICATION

Varies in height from 10–35 cm. It has three to six erect, yellow-green, sheathing base leaves, strongly keeled and with hooded tips, and several narrow, pointed stem leaves. There are 15–30 flowers in a dense cylindrical spike. The lateral sepals are erect above the tight hood formed by the dorsal sepal and two upper petals. The lip is shallowly three-lobed, with the side lobes folded tightly back, making it appear very narrow. It is marked with a pronounced red double loop enclosing a series of dots and short lines. The spur, like that of all the marsh-orchids, is fat and conical.

Sub-species: *incarnata*

Height up to 30 cm. The leaves are unspotted. The flowers are pale flesh pink in colour. The lateral sepals are marked with loops and dots. The lip is shallowly three-lobed, with the sides strongly reflexed, and marked with a double loop in red.

CONFUSING SPECIES

The spotted-orchids can be clearly separated from marsh-orchids by their slim, parallel-sided spurs. White flowered forms of Early Marsh-orchids can be misleading, but if they occur as single individuals in a population of red or purple flowers they are very unlikely to be sub-species *ochroleuca* (*page 116*). Interestingly, on the island of Gotland in the Baltic, four sub-species (excluding sub-species *coccinea*), can be found together in the same site with no apparent intermediate forms.

HYBRIDS

Hybrids are not infrequent between the sub-species and also with Common and Heath Spotted-orchids (see photographs on *pages 161–162*), Northern (see photograph on *page 16*), Western and Narrow-leaved Marsh-orchids, and also with Fragrant Orchid.

POLLINATION

The female Red-tailed Bumblebee has been recorded regularly as a pollinator of sub-species *incarnata* and sub-species *pulchella*. Seed-set is efficient.

112

Locally abundant

Height: 10–35 cm
No. of flowers: 15–30

FLOWERING PERIOD
Mid-May to July

Orange shows the known range of the Early Marsh-orchid complex; purple shows the known range of the sub-species *incarnata*

DISTRIBUTION
Sub-species *incarnata* is widely distributed throughout Britain although it is less frequent in Ireland. It has been recorded inland as a recent coloniser of fly-ash tips in north-east England

HABITAT
Sub-species *incarnata* grows in calcareous fens and marshes, in wet meadows on alkaline soils and in alkaline upland flushes up to 450 m

CONSERVATION
This species has declined markedly in central and south-east England over the last century, mainly due to drainage and agricultural improvement

Early Marsh-orchid – sub-species *pulchella* and *coccinea*

Dactylorhiza incarnata
previously: *Orchis latifolia, Orchis incarnata* and *Orchis strictifolia*

Early Marsh-orchid is represented by five sub-species, each with a different distribution. The 'nominate' form *incarnata* is described and illustrated on the previous two pages and the sub-species *ochroleuca* and *cruenta* on page 116.

Orange shows the known range of the Early Marsh-orchid complex; purple shows the known range of the sub-species *pulchella*.

Sub-species: *pulchella*

IDENTIFICATION
In all respects similar to sub-species *incarnata* (see previous page), except that the colour of the flowers is a rich mauve-purple.

HABITAT
This is a plant of acid bogs, marshes and damp heathlands up to 400m, occasionally to be found in neutral marshes and fens. It has recently been found as a coloniser of fly-ash tips in the Lee Valley, Hertfordshire.

DISTRIBUTION
Sub-species *pulchella* is sparsely distributed throughout the British Isles, with small populations in the Ashdown Forest in Sussex, the New Forest in Hampshire, Dartmoor in Devon and particularly the west of Scotland

---

Sub-species: *coccinea*

Orange shows the known range of the Early Marsh-orchid complex; purple shows the known range of the sub-species *coccinea*.

IDENTIFICATION
This is a stocky sub-species with broader, flatter leaves than the other sub-species; the leaves are unspotted. The flowers are an intense brick-red colour, unlike that of any other British orchid. This colour tends to fade with time, but the sight of a dune slack with thousands of flowering spikes like little fat Hyacinths is something never to be forgotten.

HABITAT
It is a lowland plant, typically found in coastal grassland on calcareous shell sand, in damp dune slacks and calcareous fens. In dune slacks, it may be accompanied by Marsh Helleborines (*page 50*) and Fen Orchids (*page 84*).

Nationally Scarce

DISTRIBUTION
Sub-species *coccinea* grows abundantly in the machair grasslands of north-west Scotland and the Western Isles. It also grows in huge numbers in damp dune slacks on the coast of Wales, on Anglesey and on the east coast of Scotland in Fife. It has also been recorded as a recent coloniser of fly-ash tips in inland sites

Early Marsh-orchid – sub-species *ochroleuca* and *cruenta*

Dactylorhiza incarnata

previously: *Orchis latifolia, Orchis incarnata* and *Orchis strictifolia*

Early Marsh-orchid is represented by five sub-species, each with a different distribution. The nominate form *incarnata* is described and illustrated on page 112 and the sub-species *pulchella* and *coccinea* on page 114.

Orange shows the known range of the Early Marsh-orchid complex; purple shows the known range of the sub-species *ochroleuca*

och Sub-species: *ochroleuca*

IDENTIFICATION

This plant is taller and more lax in form than the other sub-species and can be distinguished by the straw-yellow colour of the flowers. The lip is flushed with darker yellow at the base.

HABITAT

A plant of calcareous fens in lowland Britain, where it was first recorded in Norfolk in 1936. It has proved highly sensitive to the lowering of the water table, and is on the brink of extinction in Britain.

CRITICALLY ENDANGERED

DISTRIBUTION

Sub-species *ochroleuca* has been recorded in Norfolk, Suffolk, Cambridgeshire and Hampshire, but is now reduced to one small population in East Anglia. This picture is complicated by confusion with white-flowered forms of the other sub-species, particularly ssp. *pulchella*, which can appear off-white or even yellowish.

cru Sub-species: *cruenta*

Orange shows the known range of the Early Marsh-orchid complex; purple shows the known range of the sub-species *cruenta*

IDENTIFICATION

This is the only sub-species with spotted leaves, these being heavily spotted on both surfaces of the terminal third of the leaf. The flowers are purple in colour, often heavily flecked with dark purple which extends to the bracts. The side lobes of the lip are not markedly reflexed. There are different opinions on the status of the plants from Ireland, which some authorities suggest should be described as spotted-leaved variants of sub-species *pulchella*.

HABITAT

This sub-species grows in calcareous grassland which is damp for much of the year, and on the margins of seasonal lakes (turloughs) in the limestone area of The Burren in Ireland.

ENDANGERED

DISTRIBUTION

Traditionally known from The Burren in Co. Clare, and from Mayo, sub-species *cruenta* was described for the first time in the British Isles outside Ireland in 1982 when it was found in alkaline flushed grassland near Ullapool in Wester Ross.

Southern Marsh-orchid

Dactylorhiza praetermissa

previously: *Orchis praetermissa*

Locally frequent

Height: up to 70 cm
No. of flowers: 100 or more

FLOWERING PERIOD
Early June to mid-July

IDENTIFICATION

A robust plant up to 70 cm tall, with a cluster of five to nine broad, flat, unspotted, greyish-green basal leaves. Several sheathing stem leaves grade into the bracts, which are not as long as those of Early Marsh-orchid (*pages 112–117*). The flower spike is large and can bear more than 100 flowers varying in colour from pale lilac-mauve to dark magenta. The lateral sepals are spreading, becoming erect as the flowers mature. The upper sepal and petals form a loose hood. The lip is broad, even spoon-shaped, scarcely three-lobed with a pale central zone marked with small dots and dashes which never form a symmetrical double loop. The spur is thick, finger-shaped and sometimes down-curved.

CONFUSING SPECIES

Its robust size, broad, flat, unspotted leaves and broad, flat lip lacking double loop markings are distinctive.

HYBRIDS

Hybridizes readily with both Common and Heath-spotted Orchids, with Early, Northern and Narrow-leaved Marsh-orchids, and with Fragrant Orchid. Photographs of some of these hybrids are shown on *pages 161–162*. Hybrids with the spotted-orchids give rise to plants with spotted leaves, the spots sometimes forming as rings. Plants with prominent ring spots have been named Leopard Marsh-orchids, and given various scientific names such as sub-species *pardalina* and sub-species *junialis*. They occur not infrequently in south-west England, such populations showing a homogeneity and high fertility which would not normally be expected from the F1 hybrid between Southern Marsh-orchid and Common Spotted-orchid. The same picture is seen in northern France. Until further work can be done to clarify the situation, such individuals are best regarded as hybrids.

POLLINATION

There are little published data, but Large Skipper butterflies have been seen removing pollinia. Seed-set is moderately efficient and plants divide vegetatively to form clumps.

CONSERVATION

Drainage has destroyed many colonies, especially in south-east England, but it is remarkably persistent, reappearing recently in one Sussex field 14 years after the site was ploughed – there being no other colony within 15 km.

DISTRIBUTION
Widespread in southern England northwards to north-east Yorkshire, but absent from Scotland and Ireland. Less common in south-east England, and central and north Wales. Colonies in south-west England tend to have darker-coloured flowers.

HABITAT
Although it avoids truly acid conditions, it seems able to tolerate a wide range of soils, growing in fens, wet meadows, dune slacks, calcareous marshes and on road verges, golf courses and even derelict industrial sites. Although occasionally recorded in dry areas, such as the top of chalk downs, it rarely persists in such sites.

Northern Marsh-orchid

Dactylorhiza purpurella

previously: *Orchis purpurella*

Locally abundant

Height: 10–35 cm
No. of flowers: 10–40

FLOWERING PERIOD
Late May to late July

IDENTIFICATION

Northern Marsh-orchid exists as two sub-species:

pur Sub-species: *purpurella* is a robust plant 10–35 cm tall, with four to six broad, glaucous green, sheathing basal leaves and a few sheathing, pointed stem leaves. The leaves are usually unspotted, although a few may carry fine spots near the apex of the leaf. The flower spike is dense and square topped, with 10–40 bright purple to magenta coloured flowers, which are heavily marked with dark lines and dots. The lateral sepals are erect, the upper sepal and petals forming a loose hood. The heavily marked lip is diamond-shaped, with a thick conical spur.

maj Sub-species: *majaliformis* tends to be taller and more robust than sub-species *purpurella*. The leaves and bracts are heavily spotted with dull violet. The sepals and petals are longer and pinkish-purple in colour, the lip being distinctly three-lobed.

CONFUSING SPECIES

The diamond-shaped, heavily marked lip of sub-species *purpurella* is distinctive. In Ireland, confusion with Western Marsh-orchid (*page 122*) is possible, but that species has a flat lip, distinctly broader than long (see *page 37*). Sub-species *scotica* of Western Marsh-orchid is known only from North Uist in the Outer Hebrides, and has extremely heavily marked leaves which are sometimes completely bronze in colour, and a three-lobed lip marked with loops as well as lines.

HYBRIDS

Hybridizes with Common and Heath Spotted-orchids, and less frequently with Southern and Early Marsh-orchids. Photographs of some of these hybrids are shown on *pages 161–162* and *page 16*. Hybrids with Fragrant Orchid have been recorded in Wester Ross and Banff and also with Frog Orchid.

HABITAT

Grows in neutral to base-rich soils, in dune slacks, fens, marshes and wet meadows up to an altitude of 600 m. It can also flower prolifically in old quarries and derelict industrial sites.

POLLINATION

No data are available.

CONSERVATION

There are no particular conservation concerns.

DISTRIBUTION

Sub-species *purpurella* is widely distributed in western and north-west Britain, including the Scottish isles. In Ireland, it is found mainly in the north. The one English colony, in the New Forest, Hampshire, was thought to have died out, but was rediscovered in 1999.

Sub-species *majaliformis* always grows within 100 m of the sea, in dune slacks and damp pastures. It is known from the north coast of Scotland from Caithness to Ross, from Kintyre and the Outer Hebrides, and was recently found in Cardiganshire in Wales.

Western Marsh-orchid

Dactylorhiza majalis

previously: *Orchis occidentalis*

Local, may be abundant

Height: 15–35 cm
No. of flowers: up to 40

FLOWERING PERIOD
Mid-May to end of June

IDENTIFICATION

Although a fairly well-defined species in Europe, growing both in wet marshes and on mountains up to 2,000 m, the status of this species in Britain is far from clear. Irish plants are 15–35 cm tall, with about six broad, flat basal leaves, which are usually unmarked and slightly hooded at the tips. The flower spike is dense, with up to 40 fairly large, dark reddish-purple flowers, the reddish tinge suffusing the upper stem and bracts. The strap-shaped lateral sepals are erect, the dorsal sepal and upper petals forming a loose hood. The lip is broad and flat, three-lobed, with a well defined, rounded central lobe equal to, or slightly longer than, the lateral lobes which have wavy margins. The entire surface of the lip is well marked with lines and spots in a symmetrical pattern. The spur is fat and conical.

Sub-species: *scotica*

A unique population of this sub-species was discovered in the 1980s on North Uist in the Outer Hebrides. It is a dwarf plant, 5–15 cm tall, with a few broad, bright apple-green leaves very heavily marked with violet-purple blotches, which may extend across the leaf as transverse bars, or cover the entire leaf surface. There are 10–20 large reddish-purple flowers, the broad, three-lobed lip being well marked with loops and dots. The upper stem and bracts are suffused with purple.

Sub-species: *cambrensis*

Plants described as this sub-species grow on the Welsh coast and have narrower, pointed leaves covered in fine dark spots. The flower spike is tall and dense, the flowers pale mauve and finely marked. The lip tends to be diamond-shaped rather than broad, the ill-defined central lobe forming a shallow, concave pouch. Such plants may, however, prove to be more closely allied to Northern Marsh-orchid (*page 120*).

CONFUSING SPECIES

Best distinguished from Northern Marsh-orchid, particularly ssp. *majaliformis*, by the broad, three-lobed lip.

HYBRIDS

Hybrids with Heath Spotted-orchid have been recorded in Co. Clare (see photograph on *page 162*).

POLLINATION

No data on insect pollination have been recorded.

DISTRIBUTION
Widely distributed in Ireland, especially in the west, where it can flower abundantly. Elsewhere, it is probably restricted to the small Scottish population, sub-species *scotica*, in the Outer Hebrides.

HABITAT
A lowland species in Britain, growing in damp calcareous soils, fens, marshes, wet meadows and in slightly drier areas of calcareous dune slacks. Sub-species *scotica* is restricted to coastal dune slacks.

CONSERVATION
There are no particular conservation concerns

Nationally Rare

sco

cam

Narrow-leaved Marsh-orchid

Dactylorhiza traunsteineri
previously: *Orchis traunsteineroides*

Very local

Height: 20–45 cm
No. of flowers: 7–12

FLOWERING PERIOD
Mid-May to mid-June

IDENTIFICATION

A slender, elegant marsh-orchid, often with a flexuose stem. There are two to three well-spaced, narrow leaves which do not form a basal cluster, and usually one narrow, pointed stem leaf. The leaves are normally unspotted, any spots which do occur being small and few in number. The bracts are long and purple-tinged. The flower spike is lax, with only 7–12 fairly large flowers which vary in colour from lilac to reddish-purple. The long, pointed lateral sepals are unspotted and spreading, the dorsal sepal and petals forming a loose hood projecting over the lip. The lip is three-lobed, the central lobe often being much the longest with a reflexed tip, the markings being variable, often faint and not forming a pattern. The spur is stout, conical and down-pointing. White flowered plants are unusual.

CONFUSING SPECIES

Early Marsh-orchid sub-species *pulchella* (*page 114*) can be distinguished by the sharply-reflexed sides of the lip, with a small central lobe, while the Western Marsh-orchid flower has a broader three-lobed lip (see *page 37*) and much broader leaves.

HYBRIDS

The hybrid with Southern Marsh-orchid (see photograph on *page 162*) is frequent, much more robust and tends to dominate populations to the exclusion of Narrow-leaved Marsh-orchid. Hybrids with Common (see *page 161*) and Heath Spotted-orchids and Early Marsh-orchid have all been recorded.

HABITAT

Restricted to calcareous fens and base-rich marshes and wet meadows. The habitat is distinctly wetter than that enjoyed by species such as Early and Southern Marsh-orchids, plants flourishing on the edge of reed-beds or in areas where reeds have recently been cut.

POLLINATION

No data on insect pollination have been recorded.

CONSERVATION

In East Anglia, several populations have been lost as as a consequence of the lowering of the water-table. The hybrid with Southern Marsh-orchid is frequent and fares better in the drier habitat, where no trace of one parent now remains.

DISTRIBUTION
The main centres of population are in Suffolk and Norfolk in East Anglia. In Wales, it is found on Anglesey and in Merioneth, Cardiganshire and Caernarvonshire. There are scattered records from Pembrokeshire, Hampshire, north Somerset, Yorkshire and Durham. It is widespread in Ireland, but most frequent in the north and north-east. Scottish records are mainly from the north and west in Kintyre, Ardnamurchan, and east Ross; some contested records have been reassigned to Lapland or Northern Marsh-orchid

Nationally Scarce
W(NI) Order Schedule 8

124

Lapland Marsh-orchid
Dactylorhiza lapponica

Lapland Marsh-orchid was first found in 1967 in Scotland, but it was originally thought to be a variant of Narrow-leaved Marsh-orchid, and subsequently a form of Western Marsh-orchid. Finally, in 1988, it was recognised as being the same as the species found in Scandinavia and the French, Swiss and Italian Alps, and so new to the British Isles.

IDENTIFICATION
This orchid is rather slender, 6–24 cm high, with the upper stem suffused with purple. There are two or three sheathing basal leaves, and one or two non-sheathing stem leaves, pale green in colour and uniformly covered with dark violet-brown spots, rings and blotches. The leaves may be purple-edged. There is a lax spike of 3–12 large flowers, magenta-purple or magenta-red in colour, with intensely dark coloured markings. The lateral sepals are blunt, erect and marked with dark rings, the upper sepal and petals forming a loose hood. The three-lobed lip may be flat or with the lateral lobes slightly reflexed. The centre lobe is broad, longer than the lateral lobes, with a tip which may be reflexed. The spur is broad, blunt and straight.

CONFUSING SPECIES
Narrow-leaved Marsh-orchid (*page 124*) does not have the heavily spotted leaves, nor the strikingly heavily marked flowers of Lapland Marsh-orchid.

HYBRIDS
None known.

HABITAT
Grows in base-rich hill flushes at relatively low altitude, 30–300 m, where the surrounding area is moderately acidic, with Black Bog-rush and Common Butterwort. It is tolerant of low acidity levels, and can spread onto adjacent acidic wet heathland. In the base-rich sites it may be accompanied by Narrow-leaved Marsh-orchid.

POLLINATION
No data on insect pollination are available.

CONSERVATION
Many of the sites at which this species occurs could be affected by drainage or afforestation.

Rare

Height: 6–24 cm
No. of flowers: 3–12

FLOWERING PERIOD
Late May to July

DISTRIBUTION
All the known sites are in north-west Scotland and the Western Isles, in Morvern and Ardnamurchan, Kintyre, east and west Ross-shire, Sutherland and the islands of Rhum and south Harris. All the populations are small but seem stable.

Nationally Rare
W&C Act Schedule 8

Dense-flowered Orchid

Neotinea maculata

previously: *Neotinea intacta* and *Habenaria intacta*

Rare

Height: 10–40 cm
No. of flowers: 10–35

FLOWERING PERIOD
Mid-May

IDENTIFICATION

Ranges in height from 10–40 cm, woodland plants being taller and more robust. There are two or three broad, bluish-green basal leaves which form in late autumn, and one or two sheathing stem leaves. Plants in Ireland usually have unspotted leaves and white flowers, while continental plants may have leaves marked with parallel lines of tiny red spots, such plants usually having pink flowers. There are 10–35 small flowers borne on top of large fat ovaries, which are arranged in an upright, tight spiral around the stem. The flowers twist, so that they all point in the same direction. The sepals and upper petals are pointed and closely overlapping to form a sharp-ended hood, from which projects the lip. This is three-lobed, with two slender side lobes and a longer central lobe which is forked or even trifid at the tip. The spur is short and stubby.

CONFUSING SPECIES

Whilst it superficially resembles the Small-white Orchid (*page 98*), the lips of the two species are very different in shape.

HYBRIDS

None known.

HABITAT

This species has always been associated with rocky or gravelly soils on base-rich ground, particularly the sheltered grykes between the blocks of the limestone pavement of the Burren in western Ireland. It grows also on road verges in the same area and has been recorded in calcareous sand dunes. However, several recent discoveries in Ireland have been in rocky Hazel and Ash woodland, a habitat closer to that occupied by the species in continental Europe, the theory being that in the Burren it is occupying areas which are really relict woodland.

POLLINATION

The flowers have abundant nectar, but insect pollination has not been observed. Self-pollination, probably assisted by wind dislodging the fragile pollen masses, is highly efficient.

CONSERVATION

Although lost from many Irish sites, it has been found in many new ones over recent years. Sheep and Rabbits appear to relish the plants.

DISTRIBUTION

Dense-flowered Orchid is also referred to as the Irish Orchid, and was first found in Ireland in 1864. The main centre of distribution is the Burren of Co. Clare, with recent records from east Cork, west Donegal and Co. Fermanagh (1990). A small population found at the northern tip of the Isle of Man in 1967 has not been seen since 1986.

EXTINCT IN BRITAIN

Early-purple Orchid
Orchis mascula

IDENTIFICATION

Ranges in height from 10–60 cm, with a basal cluster of four to eight shiny, oblong, blunt-tipped leaves, and two or three stem leaves. Most plants have darkly-spotted leaves, the degree of spotting being highly variable. There are 20–50 pinkish-purple flowers in a loose spike, which can be lax in woodland plants. The sepals spread upwards, almost touching above the loose hood formed by the upper sepal and blunter petals. The lip is broad, three-lobed with a notch in the central lobe, and with the crenated side lobes slightly reflexed. The centre of the lip is pale and marked with dark spots. The spur is stout, blunt and upturned. When the flowers are just opened the scent is usually sweet, like honey, but soon smells strongly of tom-cat's urine, a device which may serve to inform visiting insects that pollination has already occurred. It is normally monocarpic, depending entirely on seed for future generations, which explains the wide fluctuation in the number of flowering plants from year to year. White-flowered plants **alb** are not infrequent, and may form a high percentage of some populations, as in The Burren in Ireland; they have not been recorded in Scotland. Pink-flowered plants are less common. Plants with 'broken-coloured' flowers **brf** – pale pinkish-purple, but flecked all over with mauve spots – were first recorded in Gloucestershire in 1988, where they reappeared in 1991; such plants have also been seen in Wiltshire (1989), Kent (1991) and Sussex (2001).

CONFUSING SPECIES

Very small, dark coloured plants with unspotted leaves may superficially resemble Green-winged Orchid (*page 132*), but lack the parallel green veins on the hood of that species.

HYBRIDS

The uncommon hybrid with Green-winged Orchid was recorded in Westmorland in 1985.

POLLINATION

Buff-tailed Bumblebees frequently visit the flowers. Less common pollinators recorded are solitary bees (possibly *Eucera longicornis*) and cuckoo bees of the genus *Psithyrus* (*Bombus*).

CONSERVATION

Some populations have been lost from broad-leaved woodlands which have been cleared and replanted with conifers.

DISTRIBUTION
Widespread throughout the British Isles, especially in the southern half of England. Populations have been lost in central England and in Scotland, where it is far less common in the north-east. In Ireland it is more frequent in the north and south-west, and is prominent in The Burren.

HABITAT
Grows in a wide variety of habitats on neutral or calcareous soils, flourishing in particular in broad leaved woodland and coppices. It also grows on calcareous grassland, limestone pavement, road verges and beside damp flushes on coastal cliffs.

brf

alb

Green-winged Orchid

Orchis morio

may be re-named: *Anacamptis morio*

Local, may be abundant

Height: usually 5–15 cm
No. of flowers: 5–12

IDENTIFICATION

A compact plant 5–15 cm (rarely up to 40 cm) tall, with seven to eight blue-green, unspotted basal leaves and one or two pointed, clasping stem leaves. There are 5–12 flowers varying in colour from lilac to blackish-purple, the bracts also being flushed with purple. In most populations there are a few pink-flowered plants and about 1% with pure white flowers (alb). Plants with 'broken-coloured' (flecked) flowers have been found in Kent (1999), and a single plant with straw-coloured flowers in Sussex (1966). The broad lateral sepals are marked with six to seven green, or sometimes bronze-coloured, parallel veins which give the species the alternative name of Green-veined Orchid. The dorsal sepal and blunt upper petals form a loose hood. The lip is broad and three-lobed, with the central lobe shorter. The margins are wavy and the lateral lobes folded back. The centre of the lip is white or pale, marked with heavy, dark flecks. The spur is stout and upcurved, with a slightly inflated tip which may be notched. There is no free nectar in the spur, but sugars are stored in the spur wall. Some plants, especially those which are pale coloured, have a strong vanilla scent, while others appear to be scentless.

CONFUSING SPECIES

Small, dark-coloured Early-purple Orchids (*page 130*) with unspotted leaves may look similar, but lack the green veins on the outer sepals.

HYBRIDS

The hybrid with Early-purple Orchid was recorded in Westmorland (1985) and the hybrid with Heath Spotted-orchid near Chippenham in Wiltshire (1994).

POLLINATION

The Red-tailed Bumblebee and the bumblebee *Bombus sylvarum* act as pollinators; one bumblebee was found with 16 pollinia stuck to its head! Seed-set is poor in most colonies.

CONSERVATION

This species has been lost to ploughing and pasture improvement throughout its range. The sole Scottish site has been damaged by road improvements. However, in many places sympathetic management of churchyards and pastures has led to a substantial increase in numbers in recent years. See the *Conservation in action* section on *page 171*.

FLOWERING PERIOD

Late April to early June

DISTRIBUTION

Widely distributed in coastal Wales, central and southern England and East Anglia, but now scarce in south-west England. Occurs as far north as Westmorland and north-east Yorkshire and in one small area on the west coast of Ayrshire in Scotland. In Ireland, found mainly in the central counties, with outlying populations in west Cork in the south-west and Co. Down

HABITAT

Grassy habitats on base-rich or even mildly acidic soils: found in ancient hay meadows, unimproved pastures, sand dunes, road verges, churchyards and sometimes lawns

W(NI) Order Schedule 8

alb

Burnt Orchid

Orchis ustulata
may be re-named: *Neotinea ustulata*

IDENTIFICATION

Two distinct forms flower at different times of the year.

The **early-flowering form** **E**, which is at its best in the third week of May, is small, 5–10 cm tall, with a basal rosette of two to five broad, channelled leaves with prominent veins. There are several sheathing stem leaves and red-tinged bracts. The flower spike is cylindrical and bears 15–50 small, closely-packed flowers. The sepals and upper petals form a tight hood which is dark reddish-brown when the flowers first open, giving the appearance of being 'burned', but fading rapidly as the flowers mature. The lip is white with two rounded side lobes and a bluntly-forked central lobe, marked with discrete crimson spots. There is a short, down-curved, conical spur. The flowers are sweetly-scented.

The **late-flowering form** **L** appears in July and August after the early-flowering form has set seed. It also grows in calcareous grassland, although not necessarily south-facing, seldom occurring in the same sites as the early-flowering form. It is usually taller, 8–15 cm, as the sward in which it grows is also taller at that time of year. The red colour of the hood remains strong even in mature flowers. The lip has shorter, stubbier lobes but, more importantly, the spots are larger and the edges of the lip are usually magenta-flushed, the colour sometimes suffusing the whole lip, a feature never seen in the early-flowering form.

Plants with entirely white, unmarked lips and straw-coloured hoods are occasionally recorded. A unique population growing in a series of damp meadows in Wiltshire has flower spikes well in excess of 15 cm tall.

CONFUSING SPECIES: None.   HYBRIDS: None known.

POLLINATION

The fly *Tachina magnicornis* has been recorded frequently as a pollinator. Seed-set is moderate, but plants take over 15 years to reach flowering maturity.

CONSERVATION

This species has suffered a severe decline in the last 70 years, having been lost from 210 of the 285 ten-kilometre squares where it had been recorded. Disturbance and lack of suitable grazing have been major factors in this decline, but it also appears sensitive to extremes of temperature.

134

Rare and decreasing

Height:	usually 5–15 cm
No. of flowers:	15–50

FLOWERING PERIOD
Early: early May to June
Late: July and August

DISTRIBUTION
Principally a plant of chalk and limestone hills in the south of England, but also occurs northwards to Lincolnshire, Yorkshire, Derbyshire and Durham. Found for the first time in Wales, in Glamorgan, in 1993. Absent from Scotland and Ireland. Most populations are small, but it can flower in thousands at some sites.

HABITAT
Restricted to closely-grazed grassland on chalk and limestone which has remained uncultivated for many years. Often found on south-facing slopes, particularly along terracettes.

Nationally Scarce

Lady Orchid

Orchis purpurea

previously: *Orchis fusca*

Very local

Height: up to 100 cm
No. of flowers: up to 50

FLOWERING PERIOD
Late April to June

IDENTIFICATION

A robust orchid up to 100 cm tall, with a rosette of three to five broad, shiny leaves and several narrow, sheathing stem leaves. There can be up to 50 large flowers in a fairly dense spike. The sepals and upper petals form a broad hood, coloured by dense parallel lines and flecks of dark reddish-brown, which forms the 'Lady's bonnet'. The broad, three-lobed lip is shaped like a little figure in a crinoline, the two narrow side lobes forming the 'arms', and the broad central lobe divided into two slightly rounded, wavy-edged lobes, sometimes with a median tooth. The lip is white or pale pink, with a central cluster of crimson spots, each formed by a minute bump crowned with coloured hairs. There is a slim, pink spur. Flowers with unmarked lips are not uncommon, and there are records of completely white flowers **alb**, peloric flowers with all three petals shaped like lips, and of inverted flowers with the lip uppermost.

CONFUSING SPECIES

Both the Military (*page 138*) and Monkey Orchids (*page 140*) bear a superficial resemblance to this species, but in each case the lip shape is diagnostic.

HYBRIDS

The hybrid with Man Orchid, recorded in Kent in 1998, was new to the British Isles.

HABITAT

Found in open woodland of Beech, Ash or Hazel, rarely in open grassland, on shallow chalk or limestone soils. It tends to grow in bare ground on fairly steep slopes, often close to Yew trees. It can sometimes reappear in spectacular numbers following woodland coppicing, or the felling of trees, having remained in a vegetative, non-flowering state for many years.

POLLINATION

The commonest pollinator is the small digger wasp *Odynerus parietus* and it is possible that bees may also be involved in pollination. However, seed-set is poor at only 3–10%.

CONSERVATION

Damage by slugs and deer, particularly the introduced Muntjac, can be extensive, while illegal picking and uprooting of plants is still a risk.

DISTRIBUTION

Kent remains the most important centre of the British population, with over 100 known sites in the north and east of the county. It was re-discovered in Oxfordshire in 1961; a second site found in 1999 may be an introduction. It was found recently in the Avon Gorge in Somerset (1990) and north Hampshire (2003). It last flowered in Surrey in 1959 and in Sussex in 1981.

Nationally Scarce

alb

Military Orchid
Orchis militaris

Very local

Height: 20–60 cm
No. of flowers: usually *ca.* 30

IDENTIFICATION
Usually quite robust, 20–60 cm tall, with four to five broad, shiny basal leaves with marked parallel veins, and one or two sheathing stem leaves. The bracts are small and pinkish. Most plants have about 30 flowers, but one in Suffolk was found with 115. The sepals and upper petals form a long, pointed hood. This is pale on the outside, and lilac-rose on the inner surface marked with parallel lines of mauve or dark green. The pinkish lip is long, with tufts of mauve-coloured hairs forming lines of spots down the middle – the 'buttons on the soldier's tunic'. The two side lobes, tinged pinkish-mauve, are long and narrow, curving outwards and forwards. The main body of the lip is divided into two square-cut lobes, sometimes with a median tooth. The spur is pink, rounded and down-curved. There is great variation in lip shape and markings. The flowers have a vanilla scent.

CONFUSING SPECIES
Both Lady (*page 136*) and Monkey Orchids (*page 140*) can be distinguished from Military Orchid by the shape of their lips.

HYBRIDS
The hybrid with Monkey Orchid was recorded near Pangbourne in the Thames valley years ago, when both species grew there in reasonable numbers (see photograph 14 on *page 162*).

HABITAT
Grows in chalk grassland, along the edge of broad-leaved woodland and in sunny clearings, and in scrub amongst brambles and Dog's Mercury. It has also been found on the floor of a mossy, abandoned chalk quarry in heavy shade.

POLLINATION
A great deal of fieldwork has been done to try to identify the insect pollinators. These include the solitary bees *Nomada striata* and possibly *N. flava*. In addition, leaf-cutter bees *Megachile* spp., Honeybees and bees of the genus *Andrena* may be involved. The fly *Thricops semicinerea* has been photographed with pollinia attached. Seed-set is poor.

CONSERVATION
All sites are protected, managed and carefully monitored to prevent habitat destruction and ill-intentioned collection. Slug damage is a continual hazard.

FLOWERING PERIOD
Mid-May to mid June

DISTRIBUTION
Following old records from Kent in 1836 (only proven in 1998, when the herbarium sheet was found), Essex, Middlesex, Hertfordshire, east Sussex (1934 unproven) and Berkshire, Military Orchid was thought to be extinct in Britain by the 1930s. However, it was discovered in Buckinghamshire by J. E. Lousley in 1947. A large population was then found during survey work in Suffolk in 1954. Currently, there are two sites in Oxfordshire, one in Buckinghamshire, and one in Suffolk.

VULNERABLE
W&C Act Schedule 8

Monkey Orchid
Orchis simia

Very local

Height: 10–30 cm
No. of flowers: up to 35

IDENTIFICATION

FLOWERING PERIOD
Late May to early June

The flower spike is 10–30 cm tall, with three to four blunt, glossy basal leaves, which are frequently keeled, and two or three sheathing stem leaves. The flower spike is unique among British orchids as it opens from the top downwards, giving the plant a rather untidy appearance. The sepals and petals form a long, pointed hood, white in colour tinged with lilac-rose, the hood being more spreading than that of the Military Orchid (*page 138*). It is marked with mauve dots and streaks which do not form lines. The lip has four narrow lobes that curl forwards, and a long median tooth, all tinged pinkish-mauve – the 'paws and tail of the monkey'. The base of the lip is pale, marked with mauve spots formed by coloured hairs. The spur is pale pink and the flowers are vanilla-scented. Plants in Kent tend to be taller and more robust than those in Oxfordshire, with darker flowers **drk**, and are genetically closer to those found in continental Europe.

CONFUSING SPECIES
Lady (*page 136*) and Military Orchids (*page 138*) can both be distinguished from Monkey Orchid by the shape of the lip.

HYBRIDS
The hybrid with Military Orchid was recorded several times in the 19th Century, when the two species were not uncommon in the Thames valley (see photograph 14 on *page 162*). The hybrid with Man Orchid was found in east Kent in 1985.

HABITAT
Prefers much more open habitat than the preceding two species, growing on chalky soils in well-drained, sunny, south-facing grassland, or on the edges of woodland.

POLLINATION
The Short-tongued Bee acts as a pollinator in Oxfordshire, and an unidentified bee of the same genus (*Lasioglossum*) in Kent. Large White butterflies and flies of the genus *Scathophaga* have also been observed to remove pollinia. Hand-pollination of plants in the original east Kent site led to an increase in population from six to 205 in ten years.

CONSERVATION
Many plants have been lost as a result of ploughing of downland, and in the past many were picked or dug up. In 1933, more than 30 were picked at one of the sites in Oxfordshire.

DISTRIBUTION
Once fairly common in the Thames valley between Marlow and Wallingford, but for years seldom recorded. However, there is now a flourishing population in Oxfordshire. There is also a population in east Kent which is thriving under careful conservation management. Plants found at Spurn Point in south-east Yorkshire in 1974, flowered until 1983 when the colony was lost to coastal erosion. The species also once occurred in Surrey, Berkshire and west Kent.

VULNERABLE
W&C Act Schedule 8

drk

Man Orchid

Aceras anthropophorum

may be re-named: *Orchis anthropophora*

Local

Height: 15–40 cm
No. of flowers: up to 90

FLOWERING PERIOD
May and June

IDENTIFICATION

The Man Orchid has three or four blunt basal leaves, bluish-green and veined, the ends of the leaves frequently appearing scorched by flowering time. There are several leaves clasping the stem. The flower spike, 15–40 cm tall, carries up to 90 flowers arranged in an ill-defined spiral, forming a long, cylindrical inflorescence. The colour of the flowers can range from yellow-green to a rich, foxy red-brown. The sepals and upper petals form a short, tight hood, with the edges of the sepals darker in colour. The lip is shaped like a tiny pendulous human figure, the two narrow side lobes forming the arms and the long, forked central lobe forming the legs. There is occasionally a median tooth. There is no spur, but nectar may be produced in two glands at the base of the lip.

CONFUSING SPECIES

Common Twayblade (*page 72*) has been confused with Man Orchid, but that species has two very broad basal leaves and a lip with only two lobes.

HYBRIDS

The hybrids with Monkey Orchid and with Lady Orchid were recorded in Kent in 1985 and 1998 respectively.

HABITAT

Grows in calcareous grassland, but particularly in old abandoned chalkpits and limestone quarries, where it is usually found at the foot of slopes, probably in response to moisture. It also grows on road verges, and sometimes in quite dense scrub. The most northerly sites in Britain occur on oolitic limestone.

POLLINATION

Red Ants have been seen to remove pollinia, and hoverflies also visit the flowers, but their effectiveness is not known. Seed is set in a fairly high percentage of flowers.

CONSERVATION

Many downland sites in the south of England and in east Anglia have been lost to ploughing and to scrub encroachment. Several road verge colonies have also succumbed to unsympathetic management.

DISTRIBUTION

The main centre of the British population is in Kent and Surrey, with occasional small colonies westward to Sussex, Hampshire, Wiltshire and Gloucestershire. Although it has been lost from many sites in the south (e.g. from the Isle of Wight in 1983), it has been found recently in Oxfordshire, Essex (1995), Cambridgeshire, Bedfordshire, Suffolk, Norfolk and on oolitic limestone in Northamptonshire and Lincolnshire. Plants found in Warwickshire (1968) appear to have been an introduction.

Nationally Scarce

Lizard Orchid
Himantoglossum hircinum
previously: *Orchis hircina*

Height: 25–70 cm
No. of flowers: up to 80

FLOWERING PERIOD
Late June and July

IDENTIFICATION
This is a large and distinctive orchid, 25–70 cm tall, with a dramatic, untidy-looking flower spike bearing up to 80 flowers. It has four or five broad, blunt, almost fleshy leaves which form a bulky rosette in autumn, that withers by flowering time, and four to five stem leaves. The sepals and upper petals form a tight, grey-green hood bearing parallel lines of brown dots and dashes on the inner surface. The lip is three-lobed, the long curly lateral lobes purplish brown in colour, the projecting centre lobe very long, 5–6 cm, tinged with green and purple. As the flower bud opens, the lip uncurls like a watch spring, and twists as it unrolls. The base of the lip is white, marked with crimson spots. The spur is short and conical. The lip bears a fanciful resemblance to the tail and hind legs of a lizard which has taken a header into the flower. The flowers smell very strongly of goats.

CONFUSING SPECIES: None.

HYBRIDS: None known.

HABITAT
A plant of chalk grassland, occurring less frequently on limestone soils, growing also on road verges and in calcareous sand dunes, preferring a warm, south-facing aspect. It seems to have a penchant for golf-courses; out of 16 populations in southern England, six are on golf-courses. The intriguing possibility exists that seed can be spread on golfers' shoes and the wheels of golf trolleys to new sites.

POLLINATION
The flowers attract many insects, but because of their structure only bees of moderate size can act as pollinators. They seem to prefer immature or recently opened flowers, and Buff-tailed Bumblebees will force their way in. Other pollinators include the solitary bee *Colletes marginatus*, Tawny Mining Bee and Wall-mason Wasp. Seed-set is poor, even in large populations.

CONSERVATION
In the past, many plants have been dug up and removed. Lizard Orchid seems sensitive to drought, which will kill even mature plants.

DISTRIBUTION
At present restricted to the southern half of England. In the early 1900s it was found only in Kent, but then expanded its range as far as Yorkshire, retreating again after 1930. A similar expansion started in 1990, with records west to Somerset and Gloucestershire, east to Cambridgeshire and Suffolk and north to Lincolnshire. The main populations remain in east Kent, where over 3,000 occur at one site. Cambridgeshire and Sussex. The reason for this change may be linked to the warmer, wetter winters of recent years.

VULNERABLE
W&C Act Schedule 8

Fly Orchid

Ophrys insectifera

previously: *Orchis muscifera*

Uncommon

Height: 15–60 cm

No. of flowers: usually 2–10

FLOWERING PERIOD
May and June

IDENTIFICATION

The three or four dark green, blunt, floppy basal leaves, are very shiny on the upper surface. The stem is spindly, 15–60 cm tall, and bears one or two small leaves. There are two to ten (rarely up to 20), well-spaced flowers, which bear an astonishing resemblance to an insect. The three sepals are pointed, yellow-green and stiff. The upper petals are wire-like, purple-brown and velvety, looking just like antennae. The lip is long and three-lobed, the lateral lobes rounded. The lip is rich mahogany-brown, velvety in texture, and has a brilliant band of iridescent blue – the speculum – across the middle. There are two glistening patches at the base of the lip that resemble eyes. There is a distinctive form – var. *ochroleuca* **och** – which has all-green flowers and a white speculum. Flowers with yellow-bordered lips are also occasionally recorded. Peloric flowers with multiple lips are not uncommon.

CONFUSING SPECIES: None.

HYBRIDS

The hybrid with Early Spider-orchid has been recorded in Kent, and with Bee Orchid (see photograph on *page 16*) in both Avon and West Sussex.

HABITAT

Grows in open woodland, notably the Beech 'hangers' which are a feature of the North Downs of Kent and Surrey. In northern England, it is found up to 400 m, and in Anglesey it grows in calcareous flushes and fens. It also grows on limestone pavement and on the wet margins of the seasonal lakes (turloughs) in the Burren in Ireland.

POLLINATION

The plant secretes sex pheromones that attract male Digger Wasps. The wasps attempt to copulate with the flowers, resulting in pollinia being stuck to their heads. Once the female wasps emerge, some two weeks after the males, the Fly Orchids are left alone. Ants also remove pieces of pollinia, probably as food, and may act as accidental pollinators.

CONSERVATION

Many sites were lost prior to 1930, since when it has continued to decrease due to scrub encroachment and woodland clearance.

DISTRIBUTION
In England, grows primarily in the south from Kent to Dorset, in the Cotswolds and Chilterns, north to Yorkshire and Westmorland. It grows on Anglesey in Wales, and in central Ireland and the western counties of Clare and Galway. Var. *ochroleuca* has been recorded in Hampshire, Wiltshire and Kent, and flowers with yellow-bordered lips in Surrey, Hampshire and Anglesey.

och

Early Spider-orchid

Ophrys sphegodes

previously: *Ophrys aranifera*

Local and uncommon

Height: 5–20 cm
No. of flowers: usually 3–6

FLOWERING PERIOD
Late April and May

IDENTIFICATION

Small, 5–20 cm, with three or four short, broad, grey-green basal leaves which are strongly-veined, and two or three clasping stem leaves. The flower resembles a fat, hairy spider. The sepals are large, oblong and yellow-green with wavy margins. The upper sepal curves forward over the flower. The two upper petals are strap-shaped and yellow-green with brown edges. The central lobe of the lip is round, convex, velvety in texture and rich brown in colour with a smooth blue-grey mark shaped like an 'H' in the centre. The side lobes form two golden-brown furry humps like shoulders. The column is stout, shaped like a bird's head, with a pouch on each side of the base glistening with nectar – the 'spider's eyes'. Var. *lutea* **lut** has a pale yellow lip marked with a white 'H'. and usually lacks the furry humps on the sides of the lip.

CONFUSING SPECIES: None.

HYBRIDS

The hybrid with Late Spider-orchid has been recorded in the past in Kent, and the hybrid with Fly Orchid in Kent in 1927 and several times since.

HABITAT

Traditionally found on closely-grazed chalk or limestone grassland, where it is one of the first orchids to flower in spring. For this reason, the main population centres are near the south coast of England. It also occurs rarely on disturbed coastal shingle, and has recently appeared in huge numbers on spoil from the Channel Tunnel which was spread below the Dover cliffs.

POLLINATION

Like the Fly Orchid, it attracts insect pollinators by sexual deceit. In this case it is the male Solitary Bee which gets the pollinia stuck to the front of its head. Seed-set is variable, high in Kent (nearly 100%), but poor in Sussex (6–18%). The plant has a three-year life-cycle from seed to flowering, so seed is vitally important if a population is to persist.

CONSERVATION

Lost from 12 vice-counties due to ploughing and changes in grazing management. Elsewhere it is surviving and, in one site, has spread back onto downland which had been ploughed.

DISTRIBUTION

Grows mainly in coastal areas of southern England, especially in east Kent, Sussex and Dorset, where populations may number in thousands. It has been lost recently from Hampshire (in 1971) and the Isle of Wight (in 1992), but turned up in south Wiltshire in 1988 Gloucestershire, and more surprisingly in the Breckland of Suffolk in 1991 (the first record there since 1793), and Northamptonshire in 2001 (the first record for 230 years)

Nationally Scarce
W&C Act Schedule 8

Bee Orchid

Ophrys apifera

Widespread, not uncommon

Height: 15–50 cm
No. of flowers: usually 2–7

IDENTIFICATION

This is probably our best known and well-loved orchid. There are five or six grey-green, strap-shaped basal leaves, often scorched at the tips by flowering time, two stem leaves and long, leaf-like bracts. The stem, 15–50 cm tall, bears two to seven (rarely ten) flowers. The flowers, which resemble a fat bumblebee, have three erect pink sepals, each marked with three green veins. The upper petals are brown with inrolled margins, so that they appear cylindrical. The three-lobed lip is a rich red-brown, the central lobe round and convex, velvety in texture with 'U'-shaped bands of dark brown and gold at the base. The side lobes form rounded, furry humps. The yellow apex of the lip is folded back. The column is prominent and beaked, with a fanciful resemblance to a duck's head. In this lie the two large pollinia, their caudicles running in deep grooves. There are eight distinct forms, other than the normal form, which are shown on the following two pages. Although normally monocarpic, plants have been known to flower for eight successive seasons.

CONFUSING SPECIES

Confusion with Late Spider-orchid (*page 154*), which grows only in east Kent, is unlikely, as that species has bigger flowers with triangular, orange-pink upper petals, and a square lip.

HYBRIDS

The hybrid with Fly Orchid (see *page 16*) was recorded for the first time in the wild near Bristol, where it flowered from 1968–1985. It was found for the second time in Sussex in 1998. The hybrid with the Late Spider-orchid was dubiously recorded in Kent in 1926 but may have occurred since.

HABITAT

Grows in a wide range of habitat on chalk, clay and calcareous sand, in grassland, scrub, sand dunes, limestone pavement, roadside verges, abandoned quarries and industrial waste ground where weathering has produced a base-rich substrate. Although most sites are well-drained, it can also flourish in damp areas. It is an active coloniser, sometimes appearing in large numbers on newly graded and sown road margins.

POLLINATION

Although nearly always self-pollinated, pollination by bees of the genera *Andrena* and *Eucera* may occur rarely.

FLOWERING PERIOD
June to mid July

DISTRIBUTION

Well-represented in England, especially in the south and east, north to Cumbria and Durham, but less common in the south-west. In Wales it is more often found on the coast in both the south and the north, where there is evidence that it is extending its range. In Ireland it grows mainly in central counties and the limestone country of Clare and Galway. It was believed to be extinct in Scotland, but was refound in Ayrshire in 2003.

CONSERVATION

Habitat destruction and picking still present problems.

W(NI) Order Schedule 8

150

Bee Orchid - varieties and forms
Ophrys apifera

Eight varieties and forms of the Bee Orchid have been identified in Britain. These are described and illustrated here alongside the typical form (typ).

(bic) Var. *bicolor*
The lip is divided horizontally into a pale yellow basal half and a uniform, red-brown lower half.

DISTRIBUTION: Recorded in Warwickshire, Essex and Dorset

(bel) Var. *belgarum*
The flowers are small, lack the furry side-lobes and are marked across with yellow bands.

DISTRIBUTION First described in Hampshire in 1998, now known widely from Essex to Somerset and north to Northamptonshire

(fri) Var. *friburgensis*
The two upper petals are replaced by pink, sepal-like structures, which have hairy margins.

DISTRIBUTION First found in Wiltshire in 1984, site destroyed. Since discovered in Somerset

(tro) Var. *trollii*
The lip is long and sharply-pointed, barred across with brown and yellow, lacking the furry side lobes .

DISTRIBUTION Long known from Gloucestershire, now recorded from Somerset, Dorset, Surrey Suffolk, Warwickshire and Nottinghamshire

(atr) Var. *atrofuscus*
The entire lip is a dark chocolate-brown, devoid of markings.

DISTRIBUTION Discovered in Sussex in 2001, but may have previously occurred in Hertfordshire

(chl) Var. *chlorantha*
The flowers lack the red-brown pigments, having white sepals and a greenish-yellow lip marked with white.

DISTRIBUTION Recorded in Sussex, Middlesex, Essex and Yorkshire

(Pe1) Peloric form 1
In this form, the lip is replaced by a pointed, pink structure – there is no 'bee'.

DISTRIBUTION First found and photographed in Sussex in 1919, it flowered there until destroyed by ploughing in 1940. It was subsequently refound nearby, flowering in 1969 and 1971

(Pe2) Peloric form 2
This form has all six perianth segments shaped like pink sepals, giving the flower a spurious symmetry – a condition called homeosis.

DISTRIBUTION Discovered in coastal sand dunes in Glamorgan in 1990, the plants flowered again in 1993

Late Spider-orchid

Ophrys fuciflora

previously: *Ophrys holoserica* and *Ophrys arachnites*

Rare

Height: 15–55 cm
No. of flowers: usually 2–6

FLOWERING PERIOD
End of June to mid-July

IDENTIFICATION

The three to five pointed, strap-shaped basal leaves form a rosette. They are very shiny on their upper surfaces and have well-marked veins. The flowering stem is 15–55 cm tall and bears two or three stem leaves and leaf-like bracts at the base of each flower. There are two to six (rarely eight) well-spaced, large flowers. The sepals are broad and rounded, and bright pink in colour with a dark green central vein. The upper petals are almost triangular in shape, orange-pink in colour and covered with short hairs. The lip is large, often square in outline, chestnut-brown with paler margins and velvety in texture. The side lobes of the lip form long, hairy 'shoulders', which extend down the sides of the central lobe. The pattern on the lip is complex and very variable, usually consisting of cream-coloured lines radiating from a circle. At the tip of the lip is a prominent, bright yellow appendage, which often points forwards.

CONFUSING SPECIES

Can be separated from the Bee Orchid (*pages 150–153*) by the shape and colour of the upper petals and the lip.

HYBRIDS

The hybrid with Bee Orchid is illustrated in Plate VI of *Wild Orchids of Britain* by V. S. Summerhayes (1951) but its provenance is not detailed. It has been reported several times since. The hybrid with Early Spider-orchid was recorded in Kent in 1899.

DISTRIBUTION
Restricted in recent years entirely to east Kent between Wye and Folkestone, where there are five populations which flower regularly and several which are less reliable.

HABITAT

Grows in closely-grazed grassland over well-drained chalky soil and cannot thrive in tall grass or herbage. It is often found on ancient earthworks and on the terracettes formed by sheep along the contours of steep chalk banks.

POLLINATION

There are still very little data on insect pollination in Britain, but it must occur since hybrids have been recorded with other species. In Europe, a number of insects are involved, including bees of the genus *Eucera*. Self-pollination is unlikely.

CONSERVATION (see also *page 171*)

In the past, sites have been lost to ploughing and, on some, plants have died out from a lack of appropriate grazing. All its known sites are now well-protected and efficiently managed.

VULNERABLE
W&C Act Schedule 8

Species of uncertain or doubtful provenance

Orchids are such fascinating and beautiful flowers that most botanists, if they were really honest, would wish to discover an orchid 'new to the British Isles'. This section of the book covers those species that have been recorded in Britain, but which are of uncertain or doubtful provenance. Some of these species may, however, prove to be of genuinely wild origin.

Incredibly, wild orchids are capable of migrating to Britain from continental Europe, largely because their seed is so fine that it can be carried by the wind across the English Channel. Within Europe a number of orchids have shown a northerly expansion of their range in recent years, possibly in response to changes in climate, and could well turn up in southern England. Among these possible immigrants are Short-spurred Fragrant Orchid, the tongue-orchids, and even Summer Lady's-tresses (*page 78*). In 1980, it was suggested that we should look out for the variant *friburgensis* of the Bee Orchid (*page 152*), which was showing just such a spread in northern France and Holland. In 1984 it was discovered in Wiltshire, and several years later in Somerset.

Loose-flowered Orchid is clearly the result of a recorded, carefully managed, scientific introduction, while Bertoloni's Mirror-orchid is now known to have been innocently introduced. Others have been found under circumstances which inevitably raise doubts about their authenticity, although they may ultimately be accepted on the British list. Yet others have been wrongly identified, or should be consigned to the realms of botanical myth.

Tongue-orchids – Genus: *Serapias*

All the tongue-orchids have few-flowered spikes, the hood of each flower formed by the closely adherent, pointed sepals and petals. Lip long, pointed, curved downwards, the darker coloured side lobes hidden in the hood. The base of the lip carries one or more raised bumps called calli.

⬤lin Tongue Orchid   *Serapias lingua*

IDENTIFICATION: Flower: base of lip bears single dark, purple-brown callus.

DISTRIBUTION AND BRITISH RECORDS: This species grows in western and central Mediterranean in grassland, dune slacks, olive groves and damp woodland. It was found in Guernsey in 1992. The first mainland British record, from south Devon in 1998, involved ssp. *duriuei* which is native to Algeria and Tunisia. This part of Devon is subject to occasional 'red rain' – windblown sand from the Sahara.

⬤cor Heart-flowered Tongue-orchid   *Serapias cordigera*

IDENTIFICATION: Flower: lip broad, hairy, dark brown with two diverging calli.

DISTRIBUTION AND BRITISH RECORDS: This species occurs in similar areas and habitats to the Tongue Orchid. It flowered in a chalkpit in east Kent in 1996 and again in 1997, when three plants were found. There is no evidence to suggest that it had been introduced.

156

Scarce Tongue-orchid NOT ILLUSTRATED

Serapias neglecta

IDENTIFICATION: Flower: flowers large, central lobe of lip broad-oval, hairy, marked with dark veins. Two black-purple calli.

DISTRIBUTION AND BRITISH RECORDS: Uncommon in the Mediterranean region, usually near the coast. There is only one British record, from a cornfield on the Isle of Wight in 1918.

Small-flowered Tongue-orchid

Serapias parviflora

IDENTIFICATION: Flower: flowers small, pale. Base of lip bears two small calli, close together.

DISTRIBUTION AND BRITISH RECORDS: This is the smallest-flowered of the tongue-orchids, occurring mainly in western and central Mediterranean countries. Two plants were found in flower in a coastal grassland site in east Cornwall in 1989, and others have flowered subsequently until 2001. It is possible that windblown seed from France could be the origin of the first plants, or else they may have been the result of a deliberate introduction.

Nationally Rare

Mueller's Helleborine
Epipactis muelleri

IDENTIFICATION: Resembles a spindly, small-flowered Broad-leaved Helleborine (*page 56*).

DISTRIBUTION AND BRITISH RECORDS: Occurs in south-east France, west Germany, Belgium, Holland and Switzerland. Helleborines discovered in north-east England in 1976 and 1977 were at the time thought possibly to belong to this species, but were subsequently described as Young's Helleborine (*page 58*). A similar odd population in East Sussex in 1979 proved to be depauperate specimens of Broad-leaved helleborine.

Short-spurred Fragrant-orchid
Gymnadenia odoratissima

IDENTIFICATION: Flower: smaller than Fragrant Orchid (*pages 98–101*) but paler pink and with a short spur. The scent is strong.

DISTRIBUTION AND BRITISH RECORDS: This species is widespread in mountainous regions in continental Europe, occurring in a range of habitats. There is one British record, from Black Hall Rocks in Durham in 1912, where it was growing on Magnesian limestone. The species has recently been found much further north in France than previously recorded, and could thereore spread to southern England.

Loose-flowered Orchid
Orchis laxiflora

IDENTIFICATION: Flower: resembles a loosely-packed, open spike of Southern Marsh-orchid (*page 116*), but the sides of the lip are folded back and the spur is long, slender and straight.

DISTRIBUTION AND BRITISH RECORDS: This species has long been known from both Jersey and Guernsey in the Channel Islands, where it is carefully protected. An experiment was conducted in 1987, as part of the Sainsbury Orchid Project at Kew, to see if seedling orchid plants raised in the laboratory could be transplanted successfully into the wild. This species was deliberately chosen, since it had never been recorded in Great Britain, so that, should it spread, the origin of any such plants would be known. A total of 350 seedlings were planted at Wakehurst Place in Sussex, where they have flourished.

Bertoloni's Mirror-orchid
Ophrys bertolonii

IDENTIFICATION: Flower: resembles a dark-coloured Late Spider-orchid (*page 152*). It has a blue iridescent band on the lower lip.

DISTRIBUTION AND BRITISH RECORDS: In 1976 a single plant of this beautiful orchid was found flowering on the coast of Dorset – a far cry from its usual home in the garigue country of the central Mediterranean. It was many years before it emerged that the orchid had been planted, in all innocence, by a holidaymaker returning from Italy, who felt that 'it would be happier with the other orchids'.

Calypso
Calypso bulbosa

IDENTIFICATION: Flower: usually single-flowered. The petals and sepals are pinkish-mauve, the lip bag-like and spotted orange-pink, and the spur forked.

DISTRIBUTION AND BRITISH RECORDS: This rare and beautiful orchid grows in mossy woodland in Sweden, northern Russia and across north Asia to North America. There is an unconfirmed and highly unlikely story that it was found some years ago near Scourie in east Sutherland.

Orchid hybrids recorded in Britain and Ireland

The orchid hybrids listed on this page have all been recorded in Britain and Ireland. Photographs of 18 of these hybrids are included in this book (page numbers are given):

White Helleborine *Cephalanthera damasonium* × Narrow-leaved Helleborine *C. longifolia* ......161 ①
Dark-red Helleborine *Epipactis atrorubens* × Broad-leaved Helleborine *E. helleborine*
Violet Helleborine *Epipactis purpurata* × Broad-leaved Helleborine *E. helleborine*
Broad-leaved Helleborine *Epipactis helleborine* × Narrow-lipped Helleborine *E. leptochila*
——————— × Young's Helleborine *Epipactis helleborine* var. *youngiana*
Young's Helleborine *Epipactis youngiana* × Narrow-lipped Helleborine *E. leptochila*
Narrow-lipped Helleborine *Epipactis leptochila* × Dune Helleborine *E. dunensis*
Violet Helleborine *Epipactis purpurata* × Broad-leaved Helleborine *E. helleborine*
Greater Butterfly-orchid *Platanthera chlorantha* × Lesser Butterfly-orchid *P. bifolia*
Lesser Butterfly-orchid *Platanthera bifolia* × Frog Orchid *Coeloglossum viride*
——————— × Common Spotted-orchid *Dactylorhiza fuchsii*
——————— × Heath Spotted-orchid *Dactylorhiza maculata* ssp. *ericetorum*
Pyramidal Orchid *Anacamptis pyramidalis* × Fragrant Orchid *Gymnadenia conopsea*
Small-white Orchid *Pseudorchis albida* × Fragrant Orchid *Gymnadenia conopsea*
——————— × Heath Spotted-orchid *Dactylorhiza maculata* ssp. *ericetorum*
Fragrant Orchid *Gymnadenia conopsea* × Frog Orchid *Coeloglossum viride*
——————— × Common Spotted-orchid *Dactylorhiza fuchsii* ....161 ②
——————— × Heath Spotted-orchid *Dactylorhiza maculata* ssp. *ericetorum* ....161 ③
——————— × Early Marsh-orchid *Dactylorhiza incarnata*
——————— × Southern Marsh-orchid *Dactylorhiza praetermissa*
——————— × Northern Marsh-orchid *Dactylorhiza purpurella*
Frog Orchid *Coeloglossum viride* × Common Spotted-orchid *Dactylorhiza fuchsii* ....161 ④
——————— × Heath Spotted-orchid *Dactylorhiza maculata* ssp. *ericetorum*
——————— × Southern Marsh-orchid *Dactylorhiza praetermissa*
——————— × Northern Marsh-orchid *Dactylorhiza purpurella*
Common Spotted-orchid *Dactylorhiza fuchsii* × Heath Spotted-orchid *D. maculata* ssp. *ericetorum* ...161 ⑥
——————— × Early Marsh-orchid *D. incarnata* ....161 ⑧
——————— × Southern Marsh-orchid *D. praetermissa* ....161 ⑦
——————— × Northern Marsh-orchid *D. purpurella* ....161 ⑤
——————— × Western Marsh-orchid *D. majalis*
——————— × Narrow-leaved Marsh-orchid *D. traunsteineri* ....162 ⑨
Heath Spotted-orchid *Dactylorhiza maculata* ssp. *ericetorum* × Early Marsh-orchid *D. incarnata* ...162 ⑯
——————— × Southern Marsh-orchid *D. praetermissa* ....162 ⑫
——————— × Northern Marsh-orchid *D. purpurella* ....162 ⑬
——————— × Western Marsh-orchid *D. majalis* ....162 ⑮
——————— × Narrow-leaved Marsh-orchid *D. traunsteineri*
Early Marsh-orchid *Dactylorhiza incarnata* × Southern Marsh-orchid *D. praetermissa*
——————— × Northern Marsh-orchid *D. purpurella* 16
——————— × Western Marsh-orchid *D. majalis*
——————— × Narrow-leaved Marsh-orchid *D. traunsteineri*
Southern Marsh-orchid *Dactylorhiza praetermissa* × Northern Marsh-orchid *D. purpurella* ....162 ⑪
——————— × Narrow-leaved Marsh-orchid *D. traunsteineri* ....162 ⑩
Early-purple Orchid *Orchis mascula* × Green-winged Orchid *O. morio*
Green-winged Orchid *Orchis morio* × Heath Spotted-orchid *Dactylorhiza maculata* ssp. *ericetorum*
Lady Orchid *Orchis purpurea* × Man Orchid *Aceras anthropophorum*
Military Orchid *Orchis militaris* × Monkey Orchid *O. simia* ....162 ⑭
Monkey Orchid *Orchis simia* × Man Orchid *Aceras anthropophorum*
Fly Orchid *Ophrys insectifera* × Early Spider-orchid *O. sphegodes*
——————— × Bee Orchid *O. apifera* 16
Early Spider-orchid *Ophrys sphegodes* × Late Spider-orchid *O. fuciflora*
Bee Orchid *Ophrys apifera* × Late Spider-orchid *O. fuciflora*

Status, legislation and protection

Without plants there would be no life on earth, so it is vitally important that we ensure their survival. This is being done by a combination of methods: developing an understanding of the species' status; through legislation and international agreements; by protecting places and undertaking appropriate management; through education; and by undertaking research, including the use of DNA-based analyses. This section summarises the status of Britain's wild orchids and outlines the policies and legislation that affect them. Details of the official status and relevant legal protection afforded to each species are summarised in the red "Status" boxes in the main species accounts (see *page 41*).

STATUS

The IUCN (World Conservation Union) has developed a set of criteria that are used to assess the degree to which the species is threatened. The Red Data List for vascular plants, which is included in *British Red Data Books 1: Vascular plants* uses the following categories, and includes the orchid species shown:

EXTINCT	Summer Ladies-tresses. (Dense-flowered Orchid is extinct on the Isle of Man but occurs in Ireland.)
CRITICALLY ENDANGERED	Lady's-slipper, Red Helleborine, Ghost Orchid and the sub-species *ochroleuca* of Early Marsh-orchid.
ENDANGERED	Young's Helleborine, Fen Orchid and the sub-species *cruenta* of Early Marsh-orchid.
VULNERABLE	Lizard Orchid, Military Orchid, Monkey Orchid and Late Spider-orchid.

In addition to the 'threat status', the Red Data List includes rare or scarce species which are not included in one of the IUCN categories. A species or sub-species is defined as being **Nationally Rare** if it occurs in 15 or fewer ten-kilometre squares and **Nationally Scarce** if it occurs in more than 15 but less than 100 ten-kilometre squares. The following orchid species are included in these lists:

Nationally Rare	Western Marsh-orchid, Lapland Marsh-orchid and Small-flowered Tongue-orchid.
Nationally Scarce	Dark-red Helleborine, Narrow-lipped Helleborine, Green-flowered Helleborine, Irish Ladies-tresses, Musk Orchid, the sub-species *coccinea* of Early Marsh-orchid, Narrow-leaved Marsh-orchid, Burnt Orchid, Lady Orchid, Man Orchid and Early Spider-orchid.

LEGISLATION AND PROTECTION

NATIONAL LEGISLATION

There are laws and policies in place in both the United Kingdom and Ireland to safeguard endangered or threatened species of wild plants. All plants growing in the wild belong to someone, and under the Theft Act, 1968, it is an offence in Britain to take plants for commercial use without authorisation. However, it was the plight of the Lady's-slipper which led, in part, to a law designed to protect Britain's wildlife. In 1981, the Wildlife and Countryside Act (W&C Act) made it illegal to pick or dig up any plant without the landowner's permission. It also afforded special protection to 11 orchid species, which are included in Schedule 8 (this is shown in the "Status" box of the relevant species accounts as **W&C Act Schedule 8**). These species are:

> Lady's-slipper, Red Helleborine, Young's Helleborine, Ghost Orchid, Fen Orchid, Lapland Marsh-orchid, Military Orchid, Monkey Orchid, Lizard Orchid, Early Spider-orchid and Late Spider-orchid.

In 2001, the Wildlife and Countryside Act was supplemented by the Countryside and Rights of Way (CRoW) Act, which includes a legal duty for landowners and occupiers to safeguard Biodiversity Action Plan Priority Species (see opposite) on their land.

Similar protection for plants in Northern Ireland is included in the Wildlife (Northern Ireland) Order, which was adopted in 1985. This affords special protection to eight orchid species, which are included in Schedule 8 (this is shown in the "Status" box of the relevant species accounts as **W(NI) Order Schedule 8**). These species are:

> Marsh Helleborine, Green-flowered Helleborine, Irish Lady's-tresses, Bog Orchid, Small-white Orchid, Narrow-leaved Marsh-orchid, Green-winged Orchid and Bee Orchid.

In Ireland, the key legislation is the Wildlife Act of 1976, amended in 2000. Each devolved country has its own Planning guidance which sets out how nature conservation should be taken into account in land use planning.

In the United Kingdom, a system for designating nationally important sites, including National Parks and Sites of Special Scientific Interest (SSSI), was set up in 1949. The first National Nature Reserve (NNR), the crown jewels of places for wildlife, was declared at the Kingley Vale Yew Wood in West Sussex in 1952. In Ireland, the equivalent of an SSSI is known as an Area of Special Scientific Interest (ASSI) in the North and as a Natural Heritage Area (NHA) in the Republic. In the Republic of Ireland, unlike Britain, National Parks are entirely state-owned and there is also a series of statutory nature reserves on which there is strict conservation to the exclusion of all other activities. It is worth noting that the Isle of Man and the Channel Islands are not covered by British law.

EUROPEAN LEGISLATION

Membership of the European Union (EU) has led to the implementation of some 200 pieces of environmental legislation. This includes the European Commission (EC) Habitats and Species Directive, which is designed to protect those places and species that are important in a European context. Two species of orchids which occur in Great Britain and Ireland are included in Annexes II and IV of the Directive and are afforded special protection – these are the Lady's-slipper and Fen Orchid (this is shown in the "Status" box of the relevant species accounts as **EC Habs Dir. Annexes II & IV**). The Directive also covers areas of orchid-rich grassland which support Burnt, Lady, Lizard, Man, Military, Monkey and Musk Orchids and Early and Late Spider-orchids – species which in Britain are at the northern edge of their European range. Such areas are in the process of being designated as Special Areas of Conservation (SAC). In England, the majority of the SAC sites for orchids lie on the chalk in the south-east. In Ireland, The Burren in Co. Clare and Pollardstown Fen in Co. Kildare are also in the process of becoming SACs. Further information on the Habitats and Species Directive can be obtained from the following website address: http://europa.eu.int/comm/environment/nature/legis.htm.

Other international initiatives that are relevant to orchids include legislation to prevent and control trade in endangered species. The Convention on International Trade in Endangered Species of Wild Fauna and Flora (CITES) has now been incorporated within the legislative framework of the EU. All species of UK and Irish orchids are included on it. Further information on CITES is available from the following website: www.cites.org.

In 1992, the United Nations World Summit on Sustainable Development adopted the Convention on Biological Diversity (CBD) and countries were encouraged to implement action plans for their threatened habitats and species. This was the first global agreement on the conservation and sustainable use of biological diversity. Since the mid-1990s, the UK government has published Biodiversity Action Plans (BAPs) for Priority Habitats and Species. To date, BAPs have been published for 45 habitats (Habitat Action Plans) and 391 species (Species Action Plans). The criteria for inclusion on the UKBAP list included a rapid decline over the previous 25 years. However, this could not always be shown for some species where there was insufficient information to illustrate a downward trend. Of the 66 species of flowering plant on the list, three are orchids – Lady's-slipper, Irish Lady's-tresses and Fen Orchid (this is shown in the "Status" box of the relevant species accounts as **UK BAP Priority Species**). Details of relevant websites are included in the section on *Useful addresses* on *page 180*. Ireland signed the CBD in 1992 and ratified it in 1996. The CBD is pre-eminent amongst wildlife related Conventions for widespread support and its overarching scope. In 2002, the CBD extended their interest in plants and published the Global Strategy for Plant Conservation (GSPC). This sets specific targets to halt the destruction of plant diversity at both national and international levels. The UK plan was published in 2004 and is called the Plant Diversity Challenge.

At a county level, Local Nature Reserves have been declared by local authorities, and The Wildlife Trusts have established Sites of Nature Conservation Interest (SNCI), some of which contain locally important orchid habitats. For example, at Pagham Harbour Local Nature Reserve in West Sussex, there is a damp meadow adjacent to the reserve which is full of Southern Marsh-orchids. Look out for programmes of guided walks that are run at such places and those organised by County Wildlife Trusts, the National Trust or by the conservation agencies in each of the devolved countries. These agencies are: the Countryside Council for Wales; the Environment and Heritage Service, Northern Ireland; English Nature; Scottish Natural Heritage, and the Department of the Environment, Heritage and Local Government in Ireland, which includes the National Parks and Wildlife Division and the National Heritage Service. The Botanical Society of the British Isles publishes a very useful Code of Conduct summarising the information about our plants – see the section on *Useful addresses* on *page 180*.

Many counties have adopted their own biodiversity initiatives and coordinate their own Local Biodiversity Action Plans.

Conservation in action

The activities required to safeguard our plants are many and varied. This is reflected in the following accounts of some of the key projects which are currently being undertaken. Whilst many of the projects received a welcome stimulus from government commitments to the Biodiversity Action Plan process, some have a long history, starting from the realisation that some orchids would become extinct if action was not taken. It is also clear that no one organisation can undertake this work on its own and that for some orchids conservation effort will need to be carried out in the long term. Collaboration between all the organisations and individuals involved is essential if the variety of Britain and Ireland's orchids is to be maintained for all to enjoy.

A NEW TOOL – GENETIC ANALYSIS

The use of genetic techniques is increasingly being used to enable scientists to better understand many of the issues associated with the conservation of orchids. The desire to map the human genome led to tools being developed which are relatively cheap and quick to use. These tools have, in turn, become available for the examination of other species, including plants. The analytical tools used have become highly efficient and techniques which used to take six months can now be done in a week. Over the last five years, work on orchid genetics has provided an insight into why some groups of orchids are particularly difficult to identify, and indeed how or where some groups might have originated.

Deoxyribonucleic Acid (DNA), the self-replicating material present in the chromosomes of most living organisms, provides a record of the story of evolution as much for orchids as it does for any other organism. Recent improvements in our understanding of the genetic make-up and history of orchids are beginning to influence our thinking in quite profound ways. This will probably become most obvious as changes in scientific names filter through the peer review process, reflecting our improved understanding of important aspects of orchid biology and evolution.

At the species level, one obvious impact of genetic studies has been the realisation that a similarity in appearance is not necessarily a good guide to the relationships between different orchids. Green-winged and Burnt Orchids, for example, are only distantly related to 'true' *Orchis* species such as Early-purple and Military Orchid – the former being closely allied to Pyramidal Orchid (*Anacamptis*) and the latter to Dense-flowered Orchid (*Neotinea*). There are many other examples, perhaps the most intriguing of which is the discovery that Frog Orchid seems to be a primitive type of marsh-orchid (*Dactylorhiza*). Whilst studies such as these are helping us to better appreciate how these species might have evolved, the processes driving evolution itself have also been illuminated.

Hybridisation, which is often viewed rather negatively by field botanists, has been shown to be a key mechanism in the evolution of marsh-orchids. In other genera, the processes driving evolution are more complex and have led to confusion in the interpretation of what might constitute a species. The helleborines are perhaps the best example of this and their taxonomy is once again in flux. The plants currently recognised as Young's Helleborine (*page 58*) apparently represent just part of the variable Broad-leaved Helleborine (*page 56*) gene pool, whilst the northern, dune form of Narrow-lipped Helleborine appears genetically to be a truly distinct species, Dune Helleborine (*page 62*), as does a new species referred to in this book as 'Lindisfarne' Helleborine *Epipactis sancta* (*page 64*).

A particularly interesting discovery arising from recent genetic work is that some species are capable of capturing various physiologically important cell contents from related species when hybridisation occurs. This is possible because certain cellular material (chloroplasts and mitochondria for example) are inherited only from the maternal parent. Whenever hybrids are formed, backcrossing with one of the parents is a common occurrence and can potentially result in offspring with the chloroplasts of one species and nuclear DNA very similar to another. *Orchis* species in particular seem to demonstrate this phenomenon – the evolutionary consequences being apparent if the physiological tolerances of the two parents differ significantly.

As a result of genetic investigations, changes may be made to the taxonomy and names of Britain's orchids. Possible changes to look out for in the future are detailed in the relevant individual species accounts (*pages 42-155*)

On a practical note, conservation priorities can be significantly altered if the results of genetic investigations contradict previous assumptions. In both Military and Fen Orchids, for example, it had been assumed that the largest populations were the most important to conserve in order to safeguard the species. However, genetic studies have shown that the diversity in some of the smaller populations is actually greater than in the much larger ones – significantly changing not only our understanding but also the priorities for conservation action.

RE-INTRODUCTION PROJECT – LADY'S-SLIPPER

Before the Victorian crazes for fern and orchid growing and the exchange of pressed flower specimens gathered steam, Lady's-slipper, was a widely-distributed, if thinly-spread, species on the hard limestones of northern England. By 1888, eminent botanists were already expressing concern for the plight of our most exotic flower and, in 1917, the species was declared extinct in the British Isles. However, in 1930 a single flower was re-discovered. Thankfully, there were enough conservation-minded

Lady's-slipper.

167

folk around by that time to help to safeguard this plant and its locality was kept a closely-guarded secret.

The fortunes of this single wild plant remained in the hands of a few dedicated amateur naturalists for another 30 years or so until more formal site protection measures could be put in place. A committee, the *Cypripedium* Committee, was formed to oversee its security. The plant struggled on through these years, rarely flowering and, at one point, suffering the depredations of collectors who, in their half-baked generosity, only took half the plant! Eventually, the Committee wisely determined that this knife-edge existence could not continue and that something more positive had to be done. In 1983, a generous donation from Sir Robert and Lady Salisbury enabled the establishment of the Sainsbury Orchid Conservation Project at Kew and the recovery of this beautiful species began in earnest.

Many disciplines, organisations and skilled individuals have been brought together to establish a scientifically rigorous but ambitious re-introduction project, guided in recent years by the UK Biodiversity Action Plan. Staff from the Sainsbury Orchid Conservation Project eventually cracked the secret of germinating wild-collected seed *in vitro* and re-introduction sites were identified across the former range of the species. It has taken staff from English Nature and the National Trust, together with knowledgeable volunteers from the Botanical Society of the British Isles, years to identify the right ecological conditions for the young plants from Kew. Despite this, their aftercare remains fraught with difficulties – with slugs, voles, Moles, Rabbits, deer, fungi and bacteria all taking their toll and exacerbating the problems caused by drought and competition from neighbouring vegetation. As a result, many of the re-introduced young plants have perished.

The aim is to establish at least 12 large, self-perpetuating colonies of Lady's-slipper across its former range. Each will produce hundreds, if not thousands, of flowers annually and be a delight for generations to come. To date, re-introductions have been attempted at 23 sites, and the species has gained a toehold at 11 of them. Of the 2,000 or so plants drafted into the programme, 76 have so far stood the test, with over 20 of these at a single location.

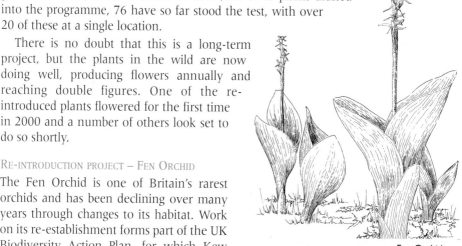

There is no doubt that this is a long-term project, but the plants in the wild are now doing well, producing flowers annually and reaching double figures. One of the re-introduced plants flowered for the first time in 2000 and a number of others look set to do so shortly.

RE-INTRODUCTION PROJECT – FEN ORCHID

The Fen Orchid is one of Britain's rarest orchids and has been declining over many years through changes to its habitat. Work on its re-establishment forms part of the UK Biodiversity Action Plan, for which Kew

Fen Orchids.

Gardens and the Norfolk Wildlife Trust are joint lead partners, and work has been undertaken in connection with English Nature's Species Recovery Programme.

In June 2000, 180 seedlings were planted in turves and re-introduced to one extant site and three former sites in East Anglia, including a Suffolk site where it had not been present for 26 years. The seedlings had been grown in the micropropagation laboratory using seeds from sites in Norfolk. The turves were cut from four sites and established in trays placed in a wooden structure lined with polythene to maintain moist conditions during the critical establishment period before being introduced to the receptor sites. In addition, an experimental planting trial that took place in 1997 of 75 continental seedlings, resulted in one plant flowering in 1999 and setting three seed-pods.

The news from a survey of all Fen Orchid sites in 2003 was mixed. Whilst the populations appear to be stable at its three major sites in East Anglia, unfortunately the introductions that occurred in 2000 in Norfolk, and at a fen in Suffolk all appear to have been unsuccessful.

SITE MANAGEMENT – NARROW-LEAVED HELLEBORINE

It appears that both Narrow-leaved and Red Helleborines like relatively high levels of light within the woodlands they inhabit (gardeners would probably use the term filtered light), but cannot tolerate too much competition. Management of sites for these orchids therefore means creating a wide range of light intensities through the selective removal of trees. The vegetation then needs to be kept in check either by mowing or by grazing at limited times of year (that is, when the plants are below ground).

Two useful examples of conservation management for this species come from Hampshire. In the east Hampshire hangers, selective removal of a few trees and bushes and the introduction of light, combined with time-limited sheep grazing, resulted in an

Narrow-leaved Helleborines.

increase from 30 to approximately 180 Narrow-leaved Helleborine plants over ten years. Over the same period, the production of seed increased from one to 85 seed-pods. At another site in Hampshire, selective felling of a copse by the Hampshire Wildlife Trust has created a woodland/glade mosaic that is now cut for hay annually. Here, the number of flowering Narrow-leaved Helleborines is in the order of 1,000 to 2,000 annually, making it the largest English population.

SITE MANAGEMENT – RED HELLEBORINE

During the course of establishing the plant conservation priorities for England, it became apparent that the criteria used to prioritise action were failing to indicate a number of species that are seriously threatened with extinction. Furthermore, some of these are species for which the conservation community in England has a high level of international responsibility. Notable amongst these species is the Red Helleborine, a stunning orchid with the most delicate pink flowers, the beauty of which, for those fortunate enough to encounter them, stays long in the memory.

The total UK population of Red Helleborine probably now numbers less than 20 plants (although some seedlings at the sites in which the plants are found are currently too small to attribute to the species with certainty). They occur in three tiny populations and are mollycoddled in the extreme – receiving that desperate level of care afforded to species believed to be on the brink of extinction. Without the dedication of site managers, County Wildlife Trust and County Council staff and volunteers over many years, that fate would almost certainly have already befallen the Red Helleborine. Had this happened, another piece of the jigsaw which makes the British countryside so enjoyable for the naturalist, would have gone, possibly forever, as this species currently appears to have very limited re-introduction potential.

But, to the future... We are now collectively aware of the risks facing Red Helleborine, of the responsibility that we have for ensuring its survival and, unfortunately, of the magnitude of that task. Seed has been collected from one of the few ripe seed-pods that has been produced and some of it has been banked at the Millennium Seed Bank situated at Wakehurst Place, part of Kew Gardens, in Sussex. Some of the seed has entered the micropropagation and genetics research programme, which is funded by English Nature and being undertaken in conjunction with partners at Kew Gardens. The remainder of the seed has been scattered on site in the hope that management activity already undertaken

Red Helleborine.

will enhance the conditions needed for germination to take place. Most importantly perhaps, all parties concerned have renewed their enthusiasm for sharing their experiences with the management of this species. We are probably going to have to be quite bold in our management regimes, recognising that with such boldness comes the risk of failure. What we must do is to ensure that lessons are learned the first time and that everyone learns together – nothing less will do if the Red Helleborine is to continue to grace our countryside.

EX-SITU CONSERVATION

The Botanic Gardens at Glasnevin in Dublin has set up an *ex-situ* collection to help conserve Irish orchids of European importance.

THE ROLE OF AGRI-ENVIRONMENT SCHEMES – GREEN-WINGED ORCHID

The Green-winged Orchid has declined steadily in Britain as a result of habitat loss. Traditional methods of managing hay meadows and pasture have fallen out of favour, with areas of grassland being ploughed up or chemically fertilised. This beautiful orchid only thrives in undisturbed hay meadows that are relatively nutrient-poor. Its future may be helped by the introduction of the Department for Environment, Food and Rural Affairs' Higher Level Environmental Stewardship Scheme, coupled with the recent introduction of the Environmental Impact Regulations for semi-natural and uncultivated land. These measures should help to safeguard and improve the management of flower-rich grasslands, but as the Green-winged Orchid is slow to become established in new sites, recovery of its former range will be a long-term process.

Green-winged Orchid meadow, Marden meadow, Kent.

Four species of orchid within the genus *Ophrys* occur in Britain – Bee and Fly Orchids, and Early and Late Spider-orchids. Of these, the Late Spider-orchid is the scarcest, its population being concentrated in Kent. This species has suffered from a loss of habitat as a consequence of agricultural improvement, loss of livestock grazing and reduced Rabbit grazing as a result of myxomatosis. A monitoring programme was set up with the aim of clarifying the plant's needs so that effective management could be implemented.

The seeds of *Ophrys* orchids are minute, consisting of an embryo composed of a few cells covered by a flattened integument which aids wind dispersal. Unlike the seeds of many plants, orchid seeds contain practically no nourishment and cannot germinate unaided. They must have the correct combination of environmental factors – light, moisture and soil pH – and the seed needs to be innoculated by a fungus of the genus *Rhizoctonia*. The mycorrhizal relationship between the orchid and the fungus is a complex and vital one.

A group of orchids was studied for 12 years, and information was gathered about the chalk grassland in which the plants grow. The analysis of the data showed that the plant:

* relies on seed for reproduction;
* produces over-wintering rosettes;
* prefers areas of broken grass sward within the chalk grassland;
* prefers soils of lower fertility;
* is an opportunist species; and
* prefers soils which drain well and places where there is air movement.

These findings have led to a modification in the intensity and timing of the grazing period and the species is thriving. Further information is contained in the English Nature Research Report 389 – *Population biology of Late Spider-orchid* Ophrys fuciflora – *a study of Wye National Nature Reserve 1987–98* by D.A. Stone and R.V. Russell (2000). This report is available free of charge from the English Nature Enquiry Service (see *page 180*).

Late Spider-orchid in protective cages.

Recording and photographing orchids

Accurate recording and mapping of plants is a vital tool in aiding the conservation and protection of our orchid species. There is no sense in having good laws for protection if we do not know where the plants are that we are trying to protect. Mapping data also enable us to monitor changes in plant populations and alert us to potential problems in the environment.

It is good practice to carry a field notebook and make notes at the time of your visit. Data should include the number of flowering plants, date of flowering, variations and abnormalities, evidence of insect pollinators, and, most importantly, an accurate site description with an equally accurate map reference or GPS (Global Positioning System) reading. The latter can be accurate to within 10m, and can become an invaluable aid in overgrown or uniform habitats where decent landmarks are lacking.

Records can be computerised, and programmes have been devised for this purpose. If you intend doing a long-term study of orchids in a particular area, it would be wise to contact your local Wildlife Trust or BSBI/County Botanical Recorder, so that you can use a compatible system. This saves hours of work – and prevents considerable frustration! See the section on Useful Addresses on *page 180*.

In the past, botanists made collections of pressed specimens on herbarium sheets and many such collections are collected in local and national museums. These make a fascinating, if sometimes chastening study when we consider what we have lost from our flora over the last 100 years. Over-collection of specimens certainly hastened the demise of some rarities, which underlines the necessity for taking great care in how we safeguard them today.

There is still a huge gap in our knowledge of the insects acting as pollinators of our wild orchids. With the development of modern 35mm digital cameras and lenses, the amateur botanist is in the position to make a genuine contribution to our understanding of this fascinating subject. However, obtaining images of sufficient quality to identify the insect for certain can be quite a challenge.

Surveying Green-winged Orchids at Muston Meadows NNR, Leicestershire.

The static situation and exotic diversity of orchids make them a very popular and potentially easy subject to photograph. Any camera with a macro, or close-up, mode is capable of producing an image, but for the best results a Single Lens Reflex camera with macro lens and slow, fine-grain film is recommended. Digital cameras can also produce excellent results. A tripod is essential in areas with little or no light, as this will help to keep the camera steady.

Control over the lens aperture is essential, as the depth of field is crucial, particularly if you want to get the front and back of a flower in focus. A flash will help solve a number of potential problems: it will provide a uniform light in dull conditions, freeze any movement of the subject, and increase the amount of detail on the subject. However, in some cases the results can look unnatural. For this reason, natural light is often the preferred choice for many photographers. Difficulties caused by the wrong part of the plant being illuminated can be overcome with the use of reflectors to help to channel light onto the exact area you want. For artistic shots, a back-lit subject can provide stunning results – though if the light is too strong try using a little fill-in flash to bring detail back onto the front of the subject.

Orchids can be found in a variety of habitats, offering all manner of photographic opportunities – but beware of some pitfalls. In spite of their static situation, movement can be a problem. Even on the calmest of days, the slightest breeze can move a subject too much to get the shot. Try to select a subject that is in a sheltered place or alternatively use something to shelter it. Good light allows the depth of field to be increased through the use of a small aperture, while still retaining a fast shutter speed. However, bright sunlight can burn out detail, particularly on light-coloured flowers, and can reduce subject detail. On closer examination, the flower head of an orchid can throw up the odd surprise – some predators hide amongst the flowers whilst waiting for their unsuspecting prey. Some spiders, for example, change their body colour to match their surroundings as they lay in wait, and can provide a focal point on the flower for an excellent photograph.

Courses and workshops are often run locally and are a very good way of learning about new techniques and getting the most from your photography.

Spikes of Greater Butterfly-orchid and Common Spotted-orchid.

Technical terms

Words shown in *Italics* are described elsewhere in the list of technical terms.

Acid	Water or soils with a *pH* value less than 7.
Alien	A species not native to the British Isles or Ireland.
Alkaline	Water or soils with a *pH* value greater than 7.
Allozyme(s)	Variants of enzymes with different genetic backgrounds, allowing genetic variation to be deduced.
Apex	The tip.
Autogamous	A flower which is self-pollinating.
Base-rich	Soils rich in alkaline nutrients especially calcium, potassium or magnesium.
Bract	A small leaf-like structure at the base of a flower stalk.
Bulbil	A small bulb arising on the leaf edge, or between the leaf and stem of a plant.
Bursicle	A small flap or pouch which covers the *viscidia* and prevents them from drying out.
Calcareous	Water or soils containing calcium – that is chalk or lime.
Capsule	The seed-containing structure, composed of a number of *carpels* joined together, at the base of the flower.
Callus	A thickened area on the lip of an orchid, more robust and longer than a *papilla*.
Carpel	One of the divisions of a *capsule*.
Caruncle	A bump found on the base of the lip of helleborines.
Caudicle	The stalk by which the *pollinium* is attached to the *viscidium* at its base.
Chlorophyll	The green pigment in most plant cells, which takes part in *photosynthesis*.
Chromosome	One of the basic parts of the cell nucleus which carries the inherited characteristics of the organism.
Cleistogamous	Self-pollinating within a flower which does not open fully.
Clint	Flat block, part of limestone pavement.
Coal-bing	A heap or pile of waste from a coal mine.
Column	A specialised structure in the centre of the orchid flower, the upper part of the female reproductive organ (*stigma*) and the lower part of the male reproductive organ (*stamen*).
Connivent	Converging (e.g. leaf veins).
Cotyledon	The first leaves of a plant produced by the germinating seed.
Crenated	Having shallow, rounded teeth.
Cymbidium	A *genus* of 40 species of *epiphytic* and terrestrial orchids from tropical Asia and Australia.
DNA	Deoxyribonucleic Acid, the self-replicating material present in the chromosomes of most living organisms.
Dorsal	At the back.

Ecology	The study of the relationships between living organisms, and between them and their environment.
Endemic	Native in one country or small area only.
Epichile	The outer part of the *labellum* of orchids of the *genus Epipactis*, the helleborines.
Epiphyte	A plant that grows on another plant.
F1 hybrid	The first generation offspring of a hybrid.
F2 hybrid	The second-generation resulting from crossing two F1 individuals.
Fertilisation	The process of uniting male and female reproductive cells.
Flexuous	Wavy.
Garigue	Dry, scrubby shrubland plant community of the Mediterranean area.
Genetics	The study of heredity.
Genus (pl. genera)	A grouping of species with important features in common (sharing first part of the scientific name e.g. *Dactylorhiza* or *Orchis*).
Gryke	Deep fissure between blocks of limestone pavement.
Homeosis	The replacement of one part by another caused by environmental factors leading, for example, to developmental anomalies.
Hood	The helmet shape formed by the *connivent* upper *petals* and *sepals* in certain orchid flowers.
Hybrid	An individual plant or animal resulting from a cross between two distinct *species*.
Hybridisation	The process by which a *hybrid* is formed.
Hypochile	The basal part of the *labellum* of orchids of the *genus Epipactis*, the helleborines.
Introgression:	The process of repeated back-crossing of an *F1 hybrid* with one of its parents.
Keeled	Leaves that have a distinct fold along the midrib, resembling the keel of a boat.
Labellum	The lip of the flower, in orchids, the lower of the three petals.
Lanceolate	Shaped like a lance head, tapering and pointed.
Lateral	On the side – can refer to shoots or *petals*.
Lax	Loose, not closely-packed.
Magnesian limestone	Soft rock formed 120 million years ago, containing magnesium oxides.
Monocarpic	Pertaining to plants that flower once and then die.
Monocotyledon	One of the two subdivisions of the flowering plants, with only one first leaf (*cotyledon*) emerging from the germinating seedling.
Mycorrhiza	The fungal threads which invade the underground parts of many orchid *species*.

Mycorrhizome	The underground structure first formed when an orchid seed germinates, usually infected with *mycorrhizal* fungus.
Nominate	The species or *sub-species* that has the same name as the *genus* or *species* respectively; this is usually the first form described.
Ovary	The lower part of the female reproductive organ which contains the seeds. An ovary set below the level of attachment of sepals and petals is known as an inferior ovary.
Papilla	Small, nipple-like projection.
Pedicel	The stalk of a single flower.
Peloric	Relates to a flower with a radially symmetrical arrangement of *perianth* members, while the species normally has an asymmetrical arrangement.
Perennial	A plant living for more than two years.
Perianth	The outer non-reproductive parts of the flower, divided into an outer series (*sepals*) and an inner series (*petals*).
Petal	One of the segments of the inner whorl of the *perianth*.
pH	Scale which gives a measure of the *alkalinity* (>7) or *acidity* (<7); pH 7 is neutral.
Pheromones	Chemicals that act as sexual attractants.
Photosynthesis	The process of converting carbon dioxide and water into carbohydrates with energy from sunlight.
Phylogeny	Evolution of a plant type.
Pollination	Transfer of pollen from the male reproductive organ (*stamen*) to the female reproductive organ (*stigma*).
Pollinium (pl. pollinia)	Structure formed by the coagulation of pollen grains into a mass.
Proboscis	The elongated mouthparts of some insects.
Protocorm	Microscopic first-development stage of growth of an orchid from seed.
Pseudobulb	A bulb-like swelling of the aerial stem, not a true bulb.
Pseudocopulation	The attempt by a male insect to mate with a flower to which it has been attracted, a process by which the *pollinia* are removed and transferred to another flower. .
Raceme	An unbranched flower *spike* where the flowers are borne on *pedicels*.
Reflexed	Folded back.
Rhizome	An underground stem, usually growing horizontally.
Rosette	A group of leaves arranged around the base of a stem, often flat on the ground.
Rostellum	The sterile third stigma of an orchid flower, situated between the *stamens* and the two functional *stigmas*. Often long and beak-shaped, bearing the *viscidia* of the *pollinia*.
Runnel	A small stream or brook.

Saprophyte	A plant which obtains its nutrients from dead plant or animal material.
Semi-peloric	Describing a flower in which the abnormal *perianth* members give a misleading appearance of being *peloric*. In the semi-peloric Bee Orchid the *labellum* resembles the *sepals*. If it were truly *peloric* it would resemble the antenna-like upper *petals*.
Sepal	One of the segments of the outer whorl of the *perianth*.
Species	A group of individuals having characteristics in common, a division of a *genus*.
Sphingid	From family *Sphingidae*, the hawk-moths.
Spike	An elongated unbranched flower head.
Sp. (plural spp.)	Abbreviation for *species*.
Spur	An elongated pouch formed at the base of the *labellum*.
Ssp. (plural sspp.)	Abbreviation for *sub-species*.
Stamen	One of the male reproductive organs.
Staminode	Modified infertile stamen.
Stigma	The receptive upper part of the female reproductive organ.
Sub-species	A division of a *species*, distinguished only by very slight *variation*, insufficient to accord it the rank of a separate *species*
Swarm	A group of *hybrids* showing a range of characteristics between those of the parent plants.
Symbiosis	Two organisms existing together to their mutual benefit.
Syrphid	From family *Syrphidae*, the hoverflies.
Taxonomy	The principles and study of the classification of species.
Terracettes	Narrow path formed across a slope, often by grazing animals.
Tuber	A swollen part of a stem or root not persisting for more than a year, tubers of successive years not arising from one another; food stores.
Valve	One of the segments of a *capsule* which splits to allow seeds to disperse.
Variation	Difference in characteristics within a *species*.
Variety (abbrev. Var.)	A minor difference in character within a *species*.
Vector	An agent, insect or otherwise, involved in carrying pollen from one flower to another.
Vegetative	Concerned with growth and development.
Vice-county	The sub-division of a county enabling the recording of species distribution. Each vice-county has its own Recorder (see entry for BSBI in *Useful addresses* on page 180).
Viscidium (pl. viscidia)	The sticky discs at the base of the *pollinia* which glue the pollen masses on to a visiting insect.

Species mentioned in the text

INSECTS

Red Ant	*Formica fusca*
Large Skipper	*Ochlodes venata*
Small Skipper	*Thymelicus sylvestris*
Large White	*Pieris brassicae*
Silver-Y moth	*Autographa gamma*
Elephant Hawk-moth	*Deilephila elpenor*
Forester moth	*Adscita statices*
Pine Hawk-moth	*Hyloicus pinastri*
Small Elephant Hawk-moth	*Deilephila porcellus*
Six-spot Burnet moth	*Zygaena filipendulae*
Buff-tailed Bumblebee	*Bombus terrestris*
Cuckoo Bee	*Psithyrus barbutellus*
Honeybee	*Apis mellifera*
Mason Bee	*Osmia uncinata*
Red-tailed Bumblebee	*Bombus lapidarius*
Short-tongued Bee	*Lasioglossum fratellum*
Solitary Bee	*Andrena nigroaena*
Tawny Mining Bee	*Andrena fulva*
Bristle Fly	*Empis tesselata*
Cuckoo Wasp	*Vespula austraica*
Digger Wasp	*Argogorytes mystaceus*
German Wasp	*Vespula germanica*
Wall-mason Wasp	*Odynerus parietum*

MAMMALS

deer	*Cervidae*
Mole	*Talpa europaea*
Rabbit	*Oryctolagus cuniculus*
vole	*Muridae*

PLANTS

Alder	*Alnus glutinosa*
Angular Solomon's-seal	*Polygonatum odoratum*
Ash	*Fraxinus excelsior*
Autumn Squill	*Scilla autumnalis*
Baneberry	*Actaea spicata*
Beech	*Fagus sylvatica*
Bell Heather	*Erica cinerea*
Bilberry	*Vaccinium myrtillus*
birch	*Betula* spp.
Black Bog-rush	*Schoenus nigrans*
Bloody Crane's-bill	*Geranium sanguineum*
Bog Asphodel	*Narthecium ossifragum*
Bottle Sedge	*Carex rostrata*
Bramble	*Rubus frutocosus agg.*
Chestnut	*Castanea sativa*
Common Bird's-foot Trefoil	*Lotus corniculatus*
Common Butterwort	*Pinguicula vulgaris*
Common Wintergreen	*Pyrola minor*
Cornish Heath	*Erica vagans*
Cranberry	*Vaccinium oxycoccos*
Creeping Willow	*Salix repens*
Crowberry	*Empetrum nigrum*
Daisy	*Bellis perennis*
Dewberry	*Rubus caesius*
Dog's Mercury	*Mercurialis perennis*
Downy Birch	*Betula pubescens*
Dwarf Birch	*Betula nana*
Fairy Flax	*Linum catharticum*
Field Maple	*Acer campestre*
goosefoot	*Chenopodium* spp.
Harebell	*Campanula rotundifolia*
hawkweed	*Hieracium* spp.
Hazel	*Corylus avellana*
Heather	*Calluna vulgaris*
Holly	*Ilex aquifolium*
Hornbeam	*Carpinus betulus*
Hyacinth	*Muscari neglectum*
Ivy	*Hedera helix*
Juniper	*Juniperus communis*
Knapweed Broomrape	*Orobanche elatior*
Lady's-bedstraw	*Galium verum*
Larch	*Larix decidua*
Ling	*Calluna vulgaris*
Lords-and-Ladies	*Arum maculatum*
Maiden Pink	*Dianthus deltoides*
Marram Grass	*Ammophila arenaria*
Marsh Clubmoss	*Lycopodiella inundata*
Marsh Pennywort	*Hydrocotyle vulgaris*
milkwort	*Polygala* spp.
Mountain Avens	*Dryas octopetala*
oak	*Quercus* spp.
One-flowered Wintergreen	*Moneses uniflora*
pine	*Pinus* spp.
Portland Spurge	*Euphorbia portlandica*
Red Fescue	*Festuca rubra*
Round-leaved Wintergreen	*Pyrola rotundifolia*
Rowan	*Sorbus aucuparia*
Rue-leaved Saxifrage	*Saxifraga tridactylites*
Sallow	*Salix caprea*
scabious	*Dipsacaceae*
Scot's Pine	*Pinus sylvestris*
Sea Holly	*Eryngium maritimum*
Sea Spurge	*Euphorbia paralias*
Sea Stork's-bill	*Erodium maritimum*
Sessile Oak	*Quercus petraea*
Sitka Spruce	*Picea sitchensis*
Solomon's-seal	*Polygonatum multiflorum*
Spanish Catchfly	*Silene otites*
Spiked Speedwell	*Veronica spicata*
Spring Sandwort	*Minuartia verna*
Squinancywort	*Asperula cynanchica*
Sweet Chestnut	*Castanea sativa*
Sweet Gale	*Myrica gale*
thyme	*Thymus* spp.
Tor-grass	*Brachypodium pinnatum*
Twin-flower	*Linnaea borealis*
Variegated Horsetail	*Equisetum variegatum*
Water Mint	*Mentha aquatica*
whitebeam	*Sorbus* spp.
willow	*Salix* spp.
Wild Arum	*Arum maculatum*
Wood Anemone	*Anemone nemorosa*
Wood Crane's-bill	*Geranium sylvaticum*
Yellow Bird's-nest	*Monotropa hypopitys*
Yellow-wort	*Blackstonia perfoliata*
Yew	*Taxus baccata*

Useful addresses

GOVERNMENT DEPARTMENTS: UK

ENGLAND
DEPARTMENT FOR ENVIRONMENT, FOOD AND RURAL AFFAIRS (DEFRA)
Conservation Management Division, London.
Tel: 020 7238 6000
www.defra.gov.uk
Environmental Land Management Schemes in England

European Wildlife Division, Bristol.
Tel: 0117 372 8974;
email: biodiversity.defra@gtnet.gov.uk
Implementation of the UK Biodiversity Action Plan.

Contact for CITES: Global Wildlife Division – CITES Policy Branch and the CITES Enforcement Team, Bristol.
POLICY:
Tel: 0117 372 8503
email: cites.ukma@defra.gsi.gov.uk
ENFORCEMENT:
Tel: 0117 372 8524
email: wildlife.enforce@defra.gsi.gov.uk

Rural Development Service
Manages the England Rural Development Programme and gives advice on Agri-environment agreements.
www.defra.gov.uk/corporate/rds/default.asp

NORTHERN IRELAND – currently c/o Defra

WALES
Department for Environment, Planning and Countryside, the Welsh Assembly Government
Tel: 029 20 825111
or write to: NAW, Cardiff Bay, Cardiff, CF99 1NA, Cymru

SCOTLAND
Scottish Executive Environment and Rural Affairs Department (SEERAD)
Tel: 0131 556 8400
email: ceu@scotland.go.uk

COUNTRY CONSERVATION AGENCIES
Contact for all matters concerning countryside conservation wildlife legislation and Designated Sites.

Joint Nature Conservation Committee (JNCC)
Maintains an overview of plant issues across Great Britain; lists protected plants on its website, Biodiversity Action Plans and Special Areas of Conservation (SACs)
Monkstone House, City Road, Peterborough PE1 1JY.
Tel: 01733 562626
www.jncc.org.uk

Countryside Council for Wales (CCW)
Plas Penrhos, Ffordd Penrhos, Bangor, Gwynedd LL57 2LQ, Wales.
Tel: 01248 385500
www.ccw.gov.uk

English Nature
Northminster House, Peterborough PE1 1UA.
Tel: 01733 455000
www.english-nature.org.uk

Environment and Heritage Service Northern Ireland
Commonwealth House, 35 Castle Street, Belfast BT1 1GU, Northern Ireland.
Tel: 029 9025 1477
www.ehsni.gov.uk

Scottish Natural Heritage
2-3 Anderson Place, Edinburgh EG9 2AS.
Tel: 0131 446 2277
www.snh.org.uk

Countryside Agency
Contact for National Parks, Areas of Outstanding Natural Beauty and a wide range of countryside matters
John Dower House, Crescent Place, Cheltenham, Glos GL50 3RA.
Tel: 01242 521381
www.countryside.gov.uk

ORGANISATIONS WITH AN INTEREST IN PLANTS

Botanical Society of the British Isles (BSBI)
A charity whose members comprise professional and amateur botanists dedicated to the study of vascular plants and stoneworts in the UK. Has a national system of Vice County Recorders who keep records of all local sightings and can provide help and advice.

C/o Botany Department, Natural History Museum, Cromwell Road, London SW7 5BD.
Bob Ellis, Volunteers' Officer,
Tel: 01603 662260;
email: VolunteersOfficer@bsbi.org.uk
www.bsbi.org.uk

Hardy Orchid Society
Voluntary society organizes outings, produce quarterly Journal
www.hardyorchidsociety.org.uk

National Trust
Charitable body concerned with the conservation of places of historic interest and natural beauty in England, Wales and Northern Ireland.

CENTRAL OFFICE, LONDON
36 Queen Anne's Gate, London SW1H 9AS.
Tel: 0870 609 5380
www.nationaltrust.org.uk

CONSERVATION DIRECTORATE
33 Sheep Street, Cirencester, Gloucestershire, GL7 1RQ.
Tel: 01285 651818

NATIONAL TRUST, NORTHERN IRELAND
Tel: 028 9751 0721

NATIONAL TRUST FOR SCOTLAND,
28 Charlotte Square, Edinburgh EH2 4ET.
Tel: 0131 243 9300; Fax: 0131 243 9301
www.nts.org.uk

NATIONAL TRUST, WALES
Tel: 01492 860123

Plantlife International
Charitable body concerned with the conservation of wild plants and their habitats.
14 Rollestone Street, Salisbury, Wiltshire SP1 1DX.
Tel: 01722 342730
www.plantlife.org.uk

PLANTLIFE SCOTLAND
Tel: 01786 478509
email: deborah.long@plantlife.org.uk

PLANTLIFE WALES
Tel: 01248 385445
email: Trevor.dines@plantlife.org.uk

Royal Botanic Gardens:
Gardens open to the public and centres for botanical science.

EDINBURGH
20a Inverleith Row, Edinburgh EH3 5LR.
Tel: 0131 552 7171
www.rbge.org.uk

KEW
Scientific authority for plants for CITES, scientific work on orchids and there are displays in glasshouses as well as an annual Orchid show in February.
Royal Botanic Gardens, Kew, Richmond, Surrey TW9 3AB.
020 8332 5000
www.rbgkew.org.uk

AND KEW'S COUNTRY GARDEN IN WEST SUSSEX
Wakehurst Place, Ardingly, Nr Haywards Heath, West Sussex RH17 6TN.
Tel: 01444 894066

WALES
National Botanic Garden of Wales, Llanarthne, Carmarthenshire SA32 8HG.
Tel: 01558 668768
www.gardenofwales.org.uk

TRAFFIC
Works to ensure that the trade in wild plants and animals does not threaten conservation.
www.traffic.org

INFORMATION AND DATA

ARKive
Non-profit making organisation providing visual resources of 12,000 animals and plants threatened with extinction.
www.arkive.org

International Union for the Conservation of Nature, IUCN (aka World Conservation Union)
Rue Mauverney 28, CH-1196, Gland, Switzerland.
Tel: +41-22-99990000; Fax: +41 22-999 0015
email: ssc@iucn.org.
www.iucn.org   www.redlist.org

National Biodiversity Network
Partnership committed to making information about UK wildlife available via the web.
Secretariat: The Kiln, Mather Road, Newark NG24 1WT.
Tel: 01636 670090
www.nbn.org.uk

United Nations Environment Programme World Conservation Monitoring Centre
Provides information for policy and action to conserve the living world
UNEP WCMC Centre, 219c Huntingdon Road, Cambridge CB3 0DL.
Tel: +44 (0)1223 277894; Fax: +44 (0)1223 277175
www.wcmc.org.uk

Universities and research organisations:
An alphabetical list can be found on:
www.scit.wlv.ac.uk/ukinfo

World Wildlife Fund
Global conservation organization
WWF-UK, Panda House, Weyside Park, Godalming, Surrey GU7 1XR.
Tel: 01483 426444
www.wwf-uk.org

IRELAND

The Department of the Environment, Heritage manages the State's statutory responsibilities under National and European law for the protection, conservation, management and preservation of Ireland's natural and built heritage. Comprises a number of Divisions – see below.
www.environ.ie

Duchas, National Heritage Service –
Responsible for the protection and enforcement of the laws to protect natural and cultural heritage
7 Ely Place, Dublin 2.
Tel: +353 1 647 3000; Fax: +353 1 662 0283
www.ealga.ie

ENFO: national environmental service
A service of the Dept. of the Environment, Heritage and Local Government
17 St Andrew St, Dublin 2.

National Parks and Wildlife Division
Responsible for natural heritage conservation. Manages six National Parks (Glenveah, Co Donegal; Connemara, Co Galway; Owenduff, Co Mayo; The Burren, Co Clare; Kilarney, Co Kerry; Wicklow Mountains, Co Wicklow). Responsible for the designation of SACs, Natural Heritage Areas (equivalent of SSSIs), Statutory Nature Reserves – Strict conservation of plants, animals wildlife habitats to the exclusion of all other activities

National Botanic Gardens
Glasnevin, Dublin 9.
Tel: +353 1 8374388. Fax: (01) 836 0080

TEAGASC
Advisory service focused on awareness of biodiversity
19 Sandymount Avenue, Ballsbridge, Dublin 9.
Tel: +353 1 637 6000; Fax: + 353 1 688 0213.

Irish Wildlife Trust
Garden Level, 21 Northumberland Road, Dublin 4.
Tel: (+353) 01 660 4530; Fax: (+353) 01 660 4571.
email: iwt@eircom.net

THE WILDLIFE TRUSTS

The Wildlife Trusts
Concerned with the conservation of wildlife throughout the UK.
Contact for information on the 47 Wildlife Trusts.
UK Office, The Kiln, Waterside, Mather Road, Newark NG24 1WT
Tel: 01636 677711
www.wildlifetrusts.org

Alderney Wildlife Trust
Wildlife Tourism Information Centre, Victoria Street, St Anne, Alderney G79 3AA.
Tel/Fax: 01481 822935
email: alderneywildlifetrust@alderney.ws
www.alderneywildlife.org

Avon Wildlife Trust
The Wildlife Centre, 32 Jacob's Wells Road, Bristol BS8 1DR.
Tel: 0117 929 7273   Fax: 0117 9 297273
email: avonwt@cix.co.uk
www.avonwildlifetrust.org.uk

The Wildlife Trust for Bedfordshire, Cambridgeshire, Northamptonshire & Peterborough
The Manor House, Broad Street, Great Cambourne, Cambridge CB3 6DH.
Tel: 01954 713500   Fax: 01954 710051
email: cambswt@cix.co.uk
www.wildlifebcnp.org

Berkshire, Buckinghamshire & Oxfordshire Wildlife Trust
The Lodge, 1 Armstrong Road, Littlemore, Oxford OX4 4XT.
Tel: 01865 775476   Fax: 01865 711301
email: bbowt@cix.co.uk
www.bboet.org.uk

The Wildlife Trust for Birmingham & Black Country
28 Harborne Road, Edgbaston, Birmingham B15 3AA.
Tel: 0121 454 1199   Fax: 0121 454 6556
email: info@bbcwildlife.org.uk
www.bbcwildlife.org.uk

Brecknock Wildlife Trust
Lion House, Bethel Square, Brecon, Powys LD3 7AY.
Tel: 01874 625708   Fax: 01874 610552
email: brecknockwt@cix.co.uk
www.wildlifetrust.org.uk/brecknock

Cheshire Wildlife Trust
Grebe House, Reaseheath, Nantwich, Cheshire CW5 6DG.
Tel: 01270 610180   Fax: 01270 610430
email: cheshirewt@cix.co.uk
www.wildlifetrust.org.uk/cheshire

Cornwall Wildlife Trust
Five Acres, Allet, Truro, Cornwall TR4 9DJ.
Tel: 01872 273939   Fax: 01872 225476
email: info@cornwt.demon.co.uk
www.cornwallwildlifetrust.org.uk

Cumbria Wildlife Trust
Plumgarths, Crook Road,
Kendal, Cumbria LA8 8LX.
Tel: 01539 816300   Fax: 01539 816301
email: cumbriawt@cix.co.uk
www.wildlifetrust.org.uk/cumbria

Derbyshire Wildlife Trust
East Mill, Bridgefoot,
Belper, Derbyshire DE56 1XH.
Tel: 01773 881188   Fax: 01773 821826
email: enquiries@derbyshirewt.co.uk
www.derbyshirewildlifetrust.org.uk

Devon Wildlife Trust
Shirehampton House, 35-37
St David's Hill, Exeter, Devon EX4 4DA.
Tel: 01392 279244   Fax: 01392 433221
email: devonwt@cix.co.uk
www.devonwildlifetrust.org

Dorset Wildlife Trust
Brooklands Farm, Forston, Dorchester,
Dorset DT2 7AA.
Tel: 01305 264620   Fax: 01305 251120
email: dorsetwt@cix.co.uk
www.wildlifetrust.org.uk/dorset

Durham Wildlife Trust
Rainton Meadows, Chilton Moor,
Houghton-le-Spring, Tyne & Wear, DH4 6PU.
Tel: 0191 584 3112   Fax: 0191 584 3934
email: durhamwt@cix.co.uk
www.wildlifetrust.org.uk/durham

Essex Wildlife Trust
The Joan Elliot Visitor Centre, Abbotts Hall
Farm, Great Wigborough, Colchester, Essex
CO5 7RZ.
Tel: 01621 862960   Fax: 01621 862990
email: admin@essexwt.org.uk
www.essexwt.org.uk

Gloucestershire Wildlife Trust
Dulverton Building, Robinswood Hill Country
Park, Reservoir Road, Gloucester GL4 6SX.
Tel: 01452 383333   Fax: 01452 383334
email:
info@gloucestershirewildlifetrust.co.uk
www.gloucestershirewildlifetrust.co.uk

Gwent Wildlife Trust
16 White Swan Court, Church Street,
Monmouth, Gwent NP25 3NY.
Tel: 01600 715501   Fax: 01600 715832
email: gwentwildlife@cix.co.uk
www.wildlifetrust.org.uk/gwent

Hampshire & Isle of Wight Wildlife Trust
Woodside House, Woodside Road, Eastleigh,
Hampshire SO50 4ET.
Tel: 02380 613636   Fax: 02380 688900
email: feedback@hwt.org.uk
www.hwt.org.uk

Herefordshire Nature Trust
Lower House Farm, Ledbury Road, Tupsley,
Hereford HR1 1UT.
Tel: 01432 356872   Fax: 01432 275489
email: herefordwt@cix.co.uk
www.wildlifetrust.org.uk/hereford

Hertfordshire & Middlesex Wildlife Trust
Grebe House, St Michael's Street, St Albans,
Herts AL3 4SN.
Tel: 01727 858901   Fax: 01727 854542
email: info@hmwt.org
www.wildlifetrust.org.uk/herts/

The Isles of Scilly Wildlife Trust
Carn Thomas, Strand, St Marys, Isles of Scilly
TR21 0PT.
Tel/Fax 01720 422153
email: enquiries@ios-wildlifetrust.org.uk
www.ios-wildlifetrust.org.uk

Kent Wildlife Trust
Tyland Barn, Sandling, Maidstone,
Kent ME14 3BD.
Tel: 01622 662012   Fax: 01622 671390
email: info@kentwildlife.org.uk
www.kentwildlife.org.uk

The Wildlife Trust for Lancashire,
Manchester and North Merseyside
The Barn, Berkeley Drive, Bamber Bridge,
Preston, Lancs PR5 6BY.
Tel: 01772324129   Fax: 01772 628849
email: lancswt@cix.co.uk
www.wildlifetrust.org.uk/lancashire/

Leicestershire & Rutland Wildlife Trust
Brocks Hill Environment Centre,
Washbrook Lane, Oadby, Leics LE2 5JJ.
Tel: 0116 2720444   Fax: 0116 2720404
email: leicswt@cix.co.uk
www.lrwt.org.uk

Lincolnshire Wildlife Trust
Banovallum House, Manor House Street,
Horncastle, Lincolnshire LN9 5HF.
Tel: 01507 526667   Fax: 01507 525732
email: lincstrust@cix.co.uk
www.lincstrust.org.uk

London Wildlife Trust
Ground Floor, Skyline House, 200 Union Street,
London SE1 0LW.
Tel: 0207 261 0447   Fax: 0207 633 0811
email: londonwt@cix.co.uk
www.wildlifetrust.org.uk/london

Manx Wildlife Trust
Conservation Centre, The Courtyard, Tynwald
Mills, St Johns, Isle of Man IM4 3AE.
Tel: 01624 801985   Fax: 01624 801022
email: manxwt@cix.co.uk
www.wildlifetrust.org.uk/manxwt/

Montgomeryshire Wildlife Trust
Collott House, 20 Severn Street, Welshpool,
Powys SY21 7AD.
Tel: 01938 555654   Fax: 01938 556161
email: montwt@cix.co.uk
www.wildlifetrust.org.uk/montgomeryshire

Norfolk Wildlife Trust
Bewick House, 22 Thorpe Road, Norwich,
Norfolk NR1 1RY.
Tel: 01603 625540   Fax: 01603 598300
email: admin@norfolkwildlifetrust.org.uk
www.wildlifetrust.org.uk/norfolk/

Northumberland Wildlife Trust
The Garden House, St Nicholas Park, Jubilee
Road, Newcastle upon Tyne NE3 3XT.
Tel: 0191 284 6884   Fax: 0191 284 6794
email: northwildlife@cix.co.uk
www.wildlifetrust.org.uk/northumberland

North Wales Wildlife Trust
376 High Street, Bangor, Gwynedd LL57 1YE.
Tel: 01248 351541   Fax: 01248 353192
email: nwwt@cix.co.uk
www.wildlifetrust.org.uk/northwales

Nottinghamshire Wildlife Trust
The Old Ragged School, Brook Street,
Nottingham NG1 1EA.
Tel: 0115 958 8242   Fax: 0115 924 3175
email: nottswt@cix.co.uk
www.wildlifetrust.org.uk/nottinghamshire

Radnorshire Wildlife Trust
Warwick House, High Street, Llandrindod Wells,
Powys LD1 6AG.
Tel: 01597 823298   Fax: 01597 823274
email: radnorshirewt@cix.co.uk
www.waleswildlife.co.uk

Scottish Wildlife Trust
Cramond House, Kirk Cramond, Cramond
Glebe Rd, Edinburgh EH4 6NS.
Tel: 0131 312 7765   Fax: 0131 312 8705
email: scottishwt@cix.co.uk
www.swt.org.uk

Sheffield Wildlife Trust
37, Stafford Road, Sheffield S2 2SF.
Tel: 0114 263 4335   Fax: 0114 263 4345
email: sheffieldwt@cix.co.uk

Shropshire Wildlife Trust
193 Abbey Foregate, Shrewsbury, Shropshire
SY2 6AH.
Tel: 01743 284280   Fax: 01743 284281
email: shropshirewt@cix.co.uk
www.shropshirewildlifetrust.org.uk

Somerset Wildlife Trust
Fyne Court, Broomfield, Bridgwater,
Somerset TA5 2EQ.
Tel: 01823 451587   Fax: 01823 451671
email: enquiries@somersetwildlife.org
www.wildlifetrust.org.uk/somerset

Staffordshire Wildlife Trust
Wolseley Centre, Wolseley Bridge,
Nr Rugeley, Stafford ST17 0YT.
Tel: 01889 880100   Fax: 01889 880101
email: staffswt@cix.co.uk
www.staffs-wildlife.org.uk

Suffolk Wildlife Trust
Brooke House, The Green, Ashbocking, Nr
Ipswich, Suffolk IP6 9JY.
Tel: 01473 890089   Fax: 01473 890165
email: info@suffolkwildlife.cix.co.uk
www.wildlifetrust.org.uk/suffolk

Surrey Wildlife Trust
School Lane, Pirbright, Woking, Surrey
GU24 0JN.
Tel: 01483 795440   Fax: 01483 486505
email: surreywt@cix.co.uk
www.surreywildlifetrust.co.uk

Sussex Wildlife Trust
Woods Mill, Shoreham Road, Henfield,
West Sussex BN5 9SD.
Tel: 01273 492630   Fax: 01273 494500
email: enquiries@sussexwt.org.uk
www.sussexwt.org.uk

Tees Valley Wildlife Trust
Bellamy Pavilion, Kirkleatham Old Hall,
Kirkleatham, Redcar, Cleveland TS10 5NW.
Tel: 01642 759900   Fax: 01642 480401
email: teesvalleywt@cix.co.uk
www.wildlifetrust.org.uk/teesvalley

Ulster Wildlife Trust
3 New Line, Crossgar, Co. Down BT30 9EP.
Tel: 02844 830282   Fax: 02844 830888
email: info@ulsterwildlifetrust.org
www.ulsterwildlifetrust.org

Warwickshire Wildlife Trust
Brandon Marsh Nature Centre, Brandon Lane,
Coventry CV3 3GW.
Tel: 02476 302912   Fax: 02476 639556
email: warkswt@cix.co.uk
www.warwickshire-wildlife-trust.org.uk

The Wildlife Trust of South and West Wales
Nature Centre, Fountain Road, Tondu,
Bridgend, Mid Glamorgan CF32 0EH.
Tel: 01656 724100   Fax: 01656 726980
email: info@wtsww.cix.co.uk

Wiltshire Wildlife Trust
Elm Tree Court, Long Street, Devizes, Wiltshire
SN10 1NJ.
Tel: 01380 725670   Fax: 01380 729017
email: admin@wiltshirewildlife.org
www.wiltshirewildlife.org

Worcestershire Wildlife Trust
Lower Smite Farm, Smite Hill, Hindlip,
Worcestershire WR3 8SZ.
Tel: 01905 754919   Fax: 01905 755868
email: worcswt@cix.co.uk
www.worcswildlifetrust.co.uk

Yorkshire Wildlife Trust
10 Toft Green, York YO1 6JT.
Tel: 01904 659570   Fax: 01904 613467
email: yorkshirewt@cix.co.uk
www.yorkshire-wildlife-trust.org.uk

Further reading

ALLAN, B. & WOODS, P. 1993. *Wild Orchids of Scotland*. HMSO Edinburgh.

CINGEL, VAN DER N.A. 1995. *An Atlas of Orchid Pollination - European Orchids*. A.A.Balkema.

DAVIES, P. & J. & HUXLEY A. 1983. *Wild Orchids of Britain and Europe*. Chatto & Windus, The Hogarth Press, London.

ELLIS, R.G. 1983. *Flowering Plants of Wales*. National Museum of Wales.

JENKINSON, M. 1991. *Wild Orchids of Dorset*. Orchid Sundries Ltd.

JENKINSON, M. 1995. *Wild Orchids of Hampshire and the Isle of Wight*. Orchid Sundries Ltd.

LANG, D. 1980. *Orchids of Britain*. Oxford University Press

LANG, D. 1989. *A Guide to the Wild Orchids of Great Britain and Ireland*. Oxford University Press.

LANG, D. 2001. *Wild Orchids of Sussex*. Pomegranate Press, Lewes.

NATURE CONSERVANCY COUNCIL. 1998. *Guidelines for the Selection of Biological SSSIs*.

NYLEN, B. 1984. *Orkideer i Norden*. Natur och Kultur, Kristianstad, Sweden.

PRESTON, C.D., PEARMAN, D.A. & DINES, T.D. 2002. *New Atlas of the British and Irish Flora*. Oxford University Press.

RODWELL, J.S. (ED.) 1991-2000. *British Plant Communities Vols. 1-5*. Cambridge University Press.

SANFORD, M. 1991. *The Orchids of Suffolk*. Suffolk Naturalists' Society, Ipswich.

SEX, S. & SAYERS, B. 2004. *Ireland's Wild Orchids*. Ireland.

STACE, C. 1991 (1997). *New Flora of the British Isles*. Cambridge University Press.

STEEL, D. & CREED, P. 1982. *Wild Orchids of Berkshire, Buckinghamshire and Oxfordshire*. Pisces Publications, Newbury.

STEWART, A., PEARMAN, D.A. & PRESTON, C.D. 1994. *Scarce Plants in Britain*. Joint Nature Conservation Committee.

SUMMERHAYES, V.S. 1951. *Wild Orchids of Britain*. Collins.

WIGGINTON, M.J. (ED.) 1999. *British Red Data Books. 1. Vascular plants*, 3rd edition. Joint Nature Conservation Committee, Peterborough.

Acknowledgements and photographic credits

The author wishes particularly to thank the following people for their kindness in supplying information, and for their encouragement in the preparation of this book: the late Bill Havers (Chilterns Military Orchid Group), Eric Philp (Monkey Orchid *Orchis simia* in Kent), Margaret Ramsay (Head of Micropropagation Unit, Royal Botanic Gardens, Kew), Dr. Francis Rose MBE., Dr. Peter Shaw (University of Surrey Roehampton), Mrs Anne Wilks (Monkey Orchid *Orchis simia* in Kent), Andy Byfield (Biodiversity Programme Manager at Plantlife International) and both Pierre Delforge and Alain Gevaudan ('Lindisfarne' Helleborine).

Dr. Jill Sutcliffe, Ian Taylor and the Botanical Service, English Nature provided invaluable input. I would also like to thank Dylan Walker, Andy Swash and Rob Still of **WILD**Guides for their enthusiasm, help and encouragement at all stages of the project.

The production of this book was greatly assisted by the contributions from a number of photographers whose work is featured here. I would like to acknowledge the skill and patience of the following photographers who kindly allowed their work to be used: Neil Barrett, the late E.J. Bedford, Stephen Blow (English Nature), Simon Booth, Catriona Carlin, Robin Chittenden (www.harlequinpictures.co.uk), Trevor Codlin, Phil Davey, Stephen Davis, John Devries, Brendan Dunford (www.burrenbeo.com), John Geeson, Bob Gibbons (Natural Image), Chris Gibson (English Nature), Paul Glendell (English Nature), Robert Goodison, Peter Lambley, Ian Millichip, James Phillips, Mike Read, Peter Roworth, Brendan Sayers, Rob Still, Jill Sutcliffe, Andy Swash, Robert Thompson, Peter Wakely (English Nature), Peter Wilson (Natural Image) and Peter J. Wilson. Every photograph used in this book is listed in the photographic credits section below, together with the photographer's name.

Cover   **Burnt Orchid**, late-flowering form: David Lang. **Bee Orchid**: Rob Still.
Endpapers – front: **Orchid flowers**: Using photographs from within the book.
Endpapers – back: **Extinct and near extinct British orchids**:
         Summer Ladies-tresses: E.T. Bedford. **Ghost Orchid**: Andy Swash.
         Dense-flowered Orchid: Robert Thompson.
Title   **Bee Orchid**: David Lang.

FRONT SECTION

6   **Lady's-slipper**: Peter Wakeley (English Nature).
8   **Early Purple Orchids**: Andy Swash.
     Monkey Orchid, flower-head: Andy Swash.
9   **Bog Orchids**: Peter Wakeley (English Nature).
10   **Pyramidal Orchids**: Mike Read.
11   **Orchid flowers**: ILLUSTRATIONS: Rob Still.
12   **Autumn Squill**: David Lang. **Bog Asphodel**: David Lang. **Knapweed Broomrape**: David Lang.
14   **Digger Wasp** on Fly Orchid: David Lang. **Bee Orchid** flower: Stephen Davis. **Bumblebee** on Green-winged Orchid: Stephen Davis.
15   *Scathophaga* **sp. flies** on Burnt Orchid: David Lang. **Bee** *Andrena nigroaena* on Early Spider-orchid: David Lang. **Marsh Fritillary** butterfly on Northern Marsh-orchid: Stephen Davis. **Hoverfly** on Dark-red Helleborine: David Lang. **Crab-spider** *Misumena vatia* on marsh-orchid: Jill Sutcliffe.

16   **Fly × Bee Orchid**: David Lang. **Early × Northern Marsh-orchid**: David Lang.
17   **Green-winged Orchid colour forms**: Peter Wakeley (English Nature).
18   **Chalk grassland** on the South Downs, East Sussex: David Lang.
19   **Breckland grassland**: Peter Lamley. **Coastal calcareous grassland**, Purbeck,
      Dorset: David Lang.
20   **Neutral grassland** with Green-winged Orchids, Marden, Kent: Stephen Davis.
      Machair on South Uist: David Lang.
21   **Dune slacks** at Ynyslas, north Wales: David Lang.
22   **Limestone pavement** on The Burren, Co. Clare: David Lang.
23   **Limestone cliffs** at Dovedale, Derbyshire: David Lang.
      Marsh at Warnborough Green, Hampshire: Bob Gibbons (Natural Image).
24   **Redgrave and Lopham Fen**: Bob Gibbons (Natural Image).
25   **Valley bog and wet flush** on Crane's Moor, New Forest, Hampshire:
      Bob Gibbons (Natural Image).
26   **Moorland,** Rannoch Moor, Highland: David Lang. **Low montane** habitat at Tir
      Stent, Dolgellau, Gwynedd: David Lang.
27   **Early-purple Orchids** under Ash coppice, Kings Wood, Heath and Reach NNR,
      Bedfordshire: Peter Wakeley (English Nature).
28   **Caledonian Pine Forest**, Loch Maree, Highland: Bob Gibbons (Natural Image).
29   **Road verge** at Amberstone, East Sussex: David Lang. **Southern Marsh-orchids at
      post-industrial site**, Canvey Island, Essex: Chris Gibson (English Nature).

FLOWER KEY

30   **Lady's-slipper**: David Lang. **White Helleborine**: David Lang. **Narrow-leaved
      Helleborine**: David Lang. **Red Helleborine**: John Devries.
31   **Marsh Helleborine**: David Lang. **Dark-red Helleborine**: Neil Barrett. **Violet
      Helleborine**: David Lang. **Broad-leaved Helleborine**: David Lang. **Young's
      Helleborine**: David Lang. **Narrow-lipped Helleborine**: John Devries.
32   **Dune Helleborine**: David Lang. **'Lindisfarne' Helleborine**: Pierre Delforge.
      Green-flowered Helleborine: David Lang. **Ghost Orchid**: Andy Swash. **Bird's-
      nest Orchid**: David Lang. **Coralroot Orchid**: David Lang.
33   **Common Twayblade**: Bob Gibbons (Natural Image). **Lesser Twayblade**: David
      Lang. **Autumn Lady's-tresses**: Neil Barrett. **Summer Lady's-tresses**: Neil Barrett.
      Irish Lady's-tresses: David Lang. **Creeping Lady's-tresses**: Neil Barrett.
34   **Fen Orchid**: David Lang. **Bog Orchid**: David Lang. **Musk Orchid**: Robin
      Chittenden (www.harlequinpictures.co.uk). **Greater Butterfly-orchid**: David Lang.
      Lesser Butterfly-orchid: David Lang.
35   **Pyramidal Orchid**: David Lang. **Fragrant Orchid**: David Lang. **Small-white
      Orchid**: Neil Barrett. **Dense-flowered Orchid**: Robert Thompson. **Frog Orchid**:
      David Lang.
36   **Common Spotted-orchid**: Andy Swash. **Heath Spotted-orchid**: David Lang.
      Early Marsh-orchid: David Lang. **Southern Marsh-orchid**: David Lang.
      Northern Marsh-orchid: David Lang.
37   **Western Marsh-orchid**: David Lang. **Narrow-leaved Marsh-orchid**: David Lang.
      Lapland Marsh-orchid: David Lang. **Early-purple Orchid**: Andy Swash. **Green-
      winged Orchid**: David Lang.
38   **Burnt Orchid**: David Lang. **Lady Orchid**: David Lang. **Military Orchid**: David
      Lang. **Monkey Orchid**: David Lang. **Man Orchid**: Andy Swash.
39   **Lizard Orchid**: David Lang. **Fly Orchid**: David Lang. **Early Spider-orchid**: David
      Lang. **Bee Orchid**: Peter Wakeley (English Nature). **Late Spider-orchid**: David Lang.

PLATES

120 **Northern Marsh-orchid**: All photographs: David Lang.
122 **Western Marsh-orchid**: All photographs: David Lang, except ssp. *cambrensis*: Neil Barrett.
124 **Narrow-leaved Marsh-orchid**: Plant (top): David Lang. Plant (bottom): Peter Wakeley (English Nature). Spike (top): David Lang. Spike (bottom): Trevor Codlin.
126 **Lapland Marsh-orchid**: David Lang.
128 **Dense-flowered Orchid**: Plant and spike: Robert Thompson.
130 **Early-purple Orchid**: Plant: David Lang. Spike (purple): Andy Swash. Spikes (white and pink): David Lang.
132 **Green-winged Orchid**: All photographs: David Lang.
134 **Burnt Orchid**: Early-flowering form – plants: Peter Roworth (English Nature). Spike: Andy Swash. Flower: David Lang. Late-flowering form – spike: David Lang.
136 **Lady Orchid**: Plants: Peter Wakeley (English Nature). Spike: Bob Gibbons (Natural Image). Flowers: David Lang.
138 **Military Orchid**: Plant: Andy Swash. Spike and flower: David Lang.
140 **Monkey Orchid**: Plant: Andy Swash. Spike (dark): Stephen Davis. Spike (pale) and flower: David Lang.
142 **Man Orchid**: Plant: David Lang. Flower: Andy Swash.
144 **Lizard Orchid**: Plant: Andy Swash. Flower: David Lang.
146 **Fly Orchid**: All photographs: David Lang.
148 **Early Spider-orchid**: Plant: Bob Gibbons (Natural Image). Flowers: David Lang.
150 **Bee Orchid**: Plant: John Geeson. Flower (white): Robin Chittenden (harlequinpictures). Flower (side): David Lang. Flower (front): Peter Wakeley (English Nature).
152 **Bee Orchid**: Flower (normal): Peter Wakeley (English Nature). All other photographs: David Lang.
154 **Late Spider-orchid**: plant: John Devries. flower: David Lang.

UNCERTAIN/DOUBTFUL SPECIES
156 **Tongue Orchid**: Andy Swash. **Heart-flowered Tongue-orchid**: David Lang. **Small-flowered Tongue-orchid**: Andy Swash.
158 **Mueller's Helleborine**: Plant and flower: Neil Barrett. **Loose-flowered Orchid**: Peter J Wilson. **Short-spurred Fragrant-orchid**: Neil Barrett. **Bertoloni's Mirror-orchid**: Andy Swash. **Calypso**: David Lang.

HYBRIDS
161 All photographs: David Lang, apart from **Frog Orchid × Common Spotted-orchid**: Stephen Blow (English Nature).
162 All photographs: David Lang, apart from **Military Orchid × Monkey Orchid**: Neil Barrett.

OTHER SECTIONS AT THE END OF THE BOOK
167 **Lady's-slipper**: illustration: Jonathan Tyler.
168 **Fen Orchid**: illustration: Sarah Wroot.
169 **Narrow-leaved Helleborine**: John Devries.
170 **Red Helleborine**: Peter Roworth (English Nature).
172 **Green-winged Orchids**: Marden Meadow, Kent: Paul Glendell (English Nature).
172 **Late Spider Orchid** cages: Robin Chittenden (www.harlequinpictures.co.uk).
173 **Surveying Green-winged Orchids** at Muston Meadows NNR, Leicestershire: Peter Wakeley (English Nature).
174 **Greater Butterfly-orchid and Common Spotted-orchid flower spikes**: Stephen Davis.

Index of English and scientific names

This index includes the English and scientific names of all the orchid species, sub-species, varieties and hybrids mentioned in the text.

Bold red page numbers refer to the main species account; **bold black** page numbers refer to species which are not illustrated; *italicised* numbers relate to page(s) on which a photograph may be found.

Natural England has been formed by bringing together English Nature (EN), the landscape, access and recreation elements of the Countryside Agency (CA) and the environmental land management functions of the Rural Development Service (RDS).

Natural England will work for people, places and nature, to enhance biodiversity, landscapes and wildlife in rural, urban, coastal and marine areas; promoting access, recreation and public well-being, and contributing to the way natural resources are managed so that they can be enjoyed now and by future generations.

These materials were printed before Natural England was created and to minimise environmental impact, existing print stocks will be used.

To order publications or find out more visit: **www.naturalengland.org.uk**

General Enquiries 0845 600 3078